travel SCRAPBOOKS

creating albums of your trips and adventures

Memory makers

Memory Makers Books
Cincinnati, Ohio
www.memorymakersmagazine.com

 Published by Memory Makers Books, an imprint of F+W Publications, Inc., 4700 East Galbraith Road, Cincinnati, Ohio 45236. (800) 289-0963. First edition.

11 10 09 08 07 5 4 3 2 1

Distributed in Canada by Fraser Direct
100 Armstrong Avenue
Georgetown, ON, Canada L7G 5S4
Tel: (905) 877-4411

Distributed in the U.K. and Europe by David & Charles
Brunel House, Newton Abbot, Devon, TQ12 4PU, England
Tel: (+44) 1626 323200, Fax: (+44) 1626 323319
Email: postmaster@davidandcharles.co.uk

Distributed in Australia by Capricorn Link
P.O. Box 704, S. Windsor NSW, 2756 Australia
Tel: (02) 4577-3555

Library of Congress Cataloging-in-Publication Data
Travel scrapbooks : creating albums of your trips and adventures / editors of Memory Makers Books.
p. cm.
Includes index.
ISBN-13: 978-1-59963-008-3 (softcover : alk. paper)
ISBN-10: 1-59963-008-7 (softcover : alk. paper)
1. Photograph albums. 2. Travel photography. 3. Scrapbooks. 4. Memory Makers Books.
TR501.T73 2007
745.593--dc22
2006102367

Editor: Amy Glander
Art Coordinator: Eileen Aber
Production Coordinator: Matt Wagner
Cover Designer: Karla Baker
Designer: Neal Miles, Righteous Planet Design, Inc.
Photographer: Adam Leigh-Manuell and John Carrico, Alias Imaging LLC
Photo Stylist: Jan Nickum

g
h
is for
HORSE RIDES
SEAWORLD
Seaworld has quickly become our favorite theme park for many reasons. • We love the animals.
This is the view from the cottage window—you can hear the waves + the view is soothing + gorgeous.
St. Andrew's, Scotland 1996
ARRIVAL
CAIRO
DEPARTED AUSTRALIA
SYDNEY AIRPORT
26 APR 199

TABLE OF CONTENTS

8-23 Hit the OPEN ROAD

10 **Trips to Kansas** *Greta Hammond*
12 **Starting Over** *Brooke Bartimioli*
14 **European Road Trips** *Barb Hogan*
16 **Road Trip by the Numbers** *Linda Harrison*
18 **The Road Trip Home** *Eileen Aber*
20 **The Bus Diaries** *Alecia Grimm*

24-41 Savvy IN THE CITY

26 **London Expedition** *Diana Lyn McGraw*
28 **I Heart NY** *Becky Fleck*
30 **Cities of Europe** *Linda Harrison*
32 **Our Trip to Niagara Falls** *Vicki Boutin*
34 **Washington, D.C.** *Caroline Ikeji*
36 **My Favorite Cities** *May Flaum*
38 **2 Travel** *Suzy Plantamura*

42-59 Life's a BEACH

44 **Cape Hatteras** *Courtney Walsh*
46 **Moments 2 Remember** *Diana Lyn McGraw*
48 **Hawaii Postcard Album** *Caroline Ikeji*
50 **Pensacola Beach** *Michelle Van Etten*
52 **2 if by Sea** *Becky Fleck*
54 **Our Faves and Memories** *Linda Harrison*
56 **Michigan Travel Box** *Hanni Baumgartner*

60-77 A Natural ATTRACTION

62 **Have Fly Rod, Will Travel** *Becky Fleck*
64 **Maine Perfection** *Diana Lyn McGraw*
66 **Our Honeymoon (Mis)Adventure** *Courtney Walsh*
68 **Anatomy of Fly Fishing** *Becky Fleck*
70 **2007 Desk Calendar** *Suzy Plantamura*
72 **A View from the Old Course** *Barb Hogan*
74 **Whistler Vacation** *Suzy Plantamura*

78-97 Ticket TO FUN

80 **Disneyland Autograph Book** *May Flaum*
82 **Down on the Farm** *Michelle Van Etten*
84 **Spring Break** *Alecia Grimm*
86 **Carnival** *Vicki Boutin*
88 **Mote Aquarium with Grandpa** *Linda Harrison*

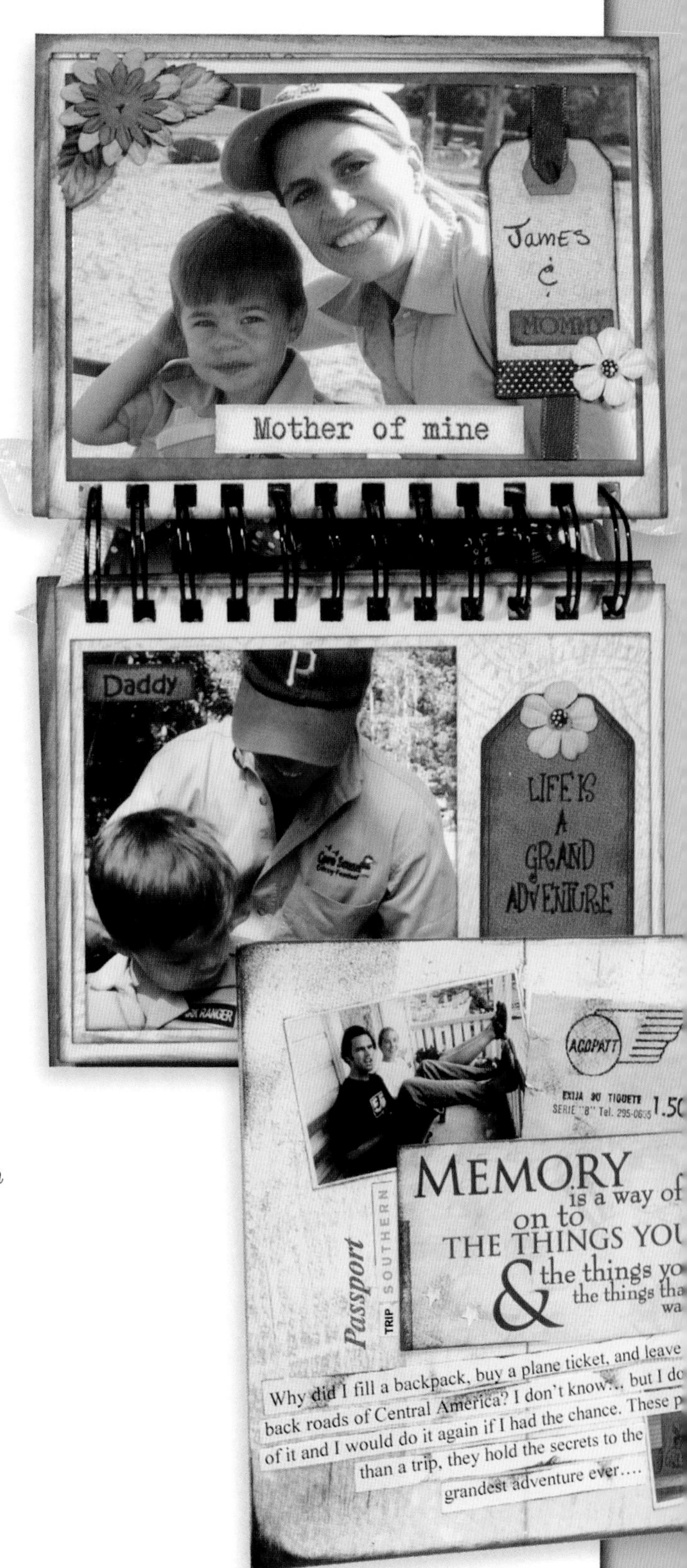

90 **Butterfly Conservatory** *Vicki Boutin*
92 **Ft. Wayne Zoo** *Greta Hammond*
94 **Chicago Children's Museum** *Courtney Walsh*
96 **Sea World** *Suzy Plantamura*

98-119 Globetrotter's Paradise

100 **Places Scrapbooking Has Taken Me** *May Flaum*
102 **The Story of Rhyolite** *Caroline Ikeji*
104 **Lazy 5 Ranch** *Michelle Van Etten*
106 **Mediterranean Summer Cruising 2000** *Vicki Boutin*
108 **Trains** *Caroline Ikeji*
110 **Bird's Eye View** *Becky Fleck*
112 **Mexico** *Alecia Grimm*
114 **Paraguay** *Alecia Grimm*
116 **Architecture Through My Lens** *Barb Hogan*

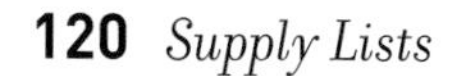

120 *Supply Lists*
125 *Source Guide*
127 *Index*

Introduction

The Roman philosopher Seneca said that traveling imparts new vigor upon the mind. If that's true, I say it doesn't matter if you're in Rome or at the tip of the South Pole—*do as the Romans do*. Perhaps you're an inquisitive tourist quick to follow your wanderlust by jetting off to exotic locales in search of the wonders of the world. Or maybe you're a day-tripper who revels in a laid-back lakeside retreat only a few hours away from home. Whatever you're destination of choice, voyaging beyond the borders of your backyard provides enrichment and fulfillment. These once-in-a-lifetime experiences deserve a place in your scrapbooks to keep them rich and colorful indefinitely.

Travel Scrapbooks will open your eyes to the creative possibilities for showing off those photos and favorite memorabilia treasures in easy-to-create travel albums. You'll find albums of every variety and format—mini, 3-ring, accordion, gatefold, post-bound, spiral-bound and more—to help you capture a journey

worth recording. You'll also find tips for colorful storytelling, creative ways to include memorabilia and expert advice for capturing amazing photos.

So if you come home with dozens of rolls of film or few spectacular postcards, turn the page for inspiration for creating extraordinary albums featuring your favorite travel destinations—whether that's the bustling streets of New York City or the sun-kissed beaches of Hawaii. It's all here inside *Travel Scrapbooks*.

Chapter one

Hit the OPEN ROAD

Do you long for cross-country adventures on two-lane highways? For some, there's nothing more exciting than climbing into the car with freewheeling friends and barreling west on the Interstate. Reaching your destination involves following the map to find roadside attractions, throwback diners, historical lore and the beauty and splendor of natural wonders. Turn the page of this chapter to find stunning examples of road trip albums that will kindle your creative fire. Discover ways to put a new twist on scrapbooks documenting annual trips, techniques for distressing album pages, unique album shapes and formats, and methods for safely storing memorabilia and other treasures within your pages. Whether you're set out to travel coast-to-coast or are simply looking for a weekend jaunt, if a road trip beckons—follow that call. A world of adventure awaits.

UNITED STATES OF AMERICA
UNITED STATES OF AMERICA
DOMINION OF CANADA
PACIFIC OCEAN
MEXICO
Gulf of Mexico
ATLANTIC OCEAN
RELIEF MAP OF THE UNITED STATES
ID
FROM
CA
MT. LYELL
13,114 FT.
MT. ANSEL ADAMS
EL 11,726 FT.
EL. 13,157 FT.
PENSKE
Local
One Way
we look
like hippies!
8 A.M.
It sounds crazy
that we bought
a house in Hayden
Idaho, when
we've lived in
Tahoe all our lives
and are making
a good, consistent
income there
Why?
A fresh
start is
very appealing
HOPE
FUL
Grand Canyon
National Park Arizona

Trips to Kansas

Greta Hammond of Goshen, Indiana

To Grandma and Grandpa's house we go! An annual family trip to see beloved grandparents in Kansas is certainly worthy of documentation. Mulberry picking, mule rides and golf lessons are only just a part of the fun. Greta records these good times in a book showing the love and laughter of this happy family.

A post-bound album is the perfect choice for displaying a wealth of family photos. A great way to show the passage of time, the growth of little ones and the change in fashions is to create album pages showing family members taking part in the same activities or traditions each year. In this example, Greta photographed her son striking a pose next to his favorite statue at the zoo. This gives the album continuity and makes it fun for viewers to see how photo subjects change from year to year. Keep your pages simple with minimal embellishments and use repeated geometric shapes to create unity and rhythm.

zoo buds
04
Every year. The same place. The same time. Just like meeting an old friend.
05

Playing golf is part of our everyday life when we are at Grandpa's house. You and Grandpa go out at least a couple of times a day, playing a few holes, driving the cart and hitting the park before you come home. Our visits wouldn't be complete without this little tradition.
golf
Lessons

nce we go to Kansas at about the same time every year, we inevitably hit either Mullberry or Dewberry
ason at Grandma and Grandpa's farm. We love to take the mule out and find the trees loaded with
rries. We pick and eat. Pick and eat. Pick and eat until our fingers, faces and sometimes bare feet are
rple and our bellies full. Such a fun summertime treat.
MullBeRRy
pIcKiNg

Starting Over

Brooke Bartimioli of Hayden, Idaho

With a packed van and faith in a new start, Brooke and her husband left their city of comfort for the unspoiled woods and lakes of Idaho. Their journey, which included multiple treks over a six-month period, was an experience worthy of documentation. To both record and celebrate their adventure, Brooke created this 7.5" x 5" (19cm x 13cm) handmade album peppered with whimsical details.

If you're going for an aged look, try applying a crackle medium. In this example, Brooke took a vintage book, removed the original pages and altered the cover with crackle medium applied over acrylic paint. She constructed her interior pages using patterned paper and photos, and then bound them together with identical punched holes woven with industrial twine. Another way to achieve an antique look is to use sepia-toned photos distressed with scratches and photo ink. These subtle details create a timeless feeling that captures the true spirit of these modern-day pioneers. Include maps, stickers, labels and other design elements to add further charm.

European Road Trips

Barb Hogan of Cincinnati, Ohio

Whether you're meandering through ancient ruins and rocky coasts in cinematic Ireland, or floating down the Grand Canal in search of Casanova in mesmerizing Venice, a road trip through Europe takes on a whole new meaning. It holds even more discovery when you move from inquisitive tourist to year-long resident. Barb captured these amazing panoramic shots during her time spent living in this endless visual playground.

If you want to document more than one city in a single album, a good choice is to keep your backgrounds free of heavy embellishment. Too many lumps and bumps and your photos get lost amongst the layers. Instead, carefully select papers that subtly coordinate in either color or pattern, and choose a shape, in this case concentric circles, to repeat for continuity. Acrylic paint works great for bold lettering while hand-drawn scrolls provide an elegant finishing touch.

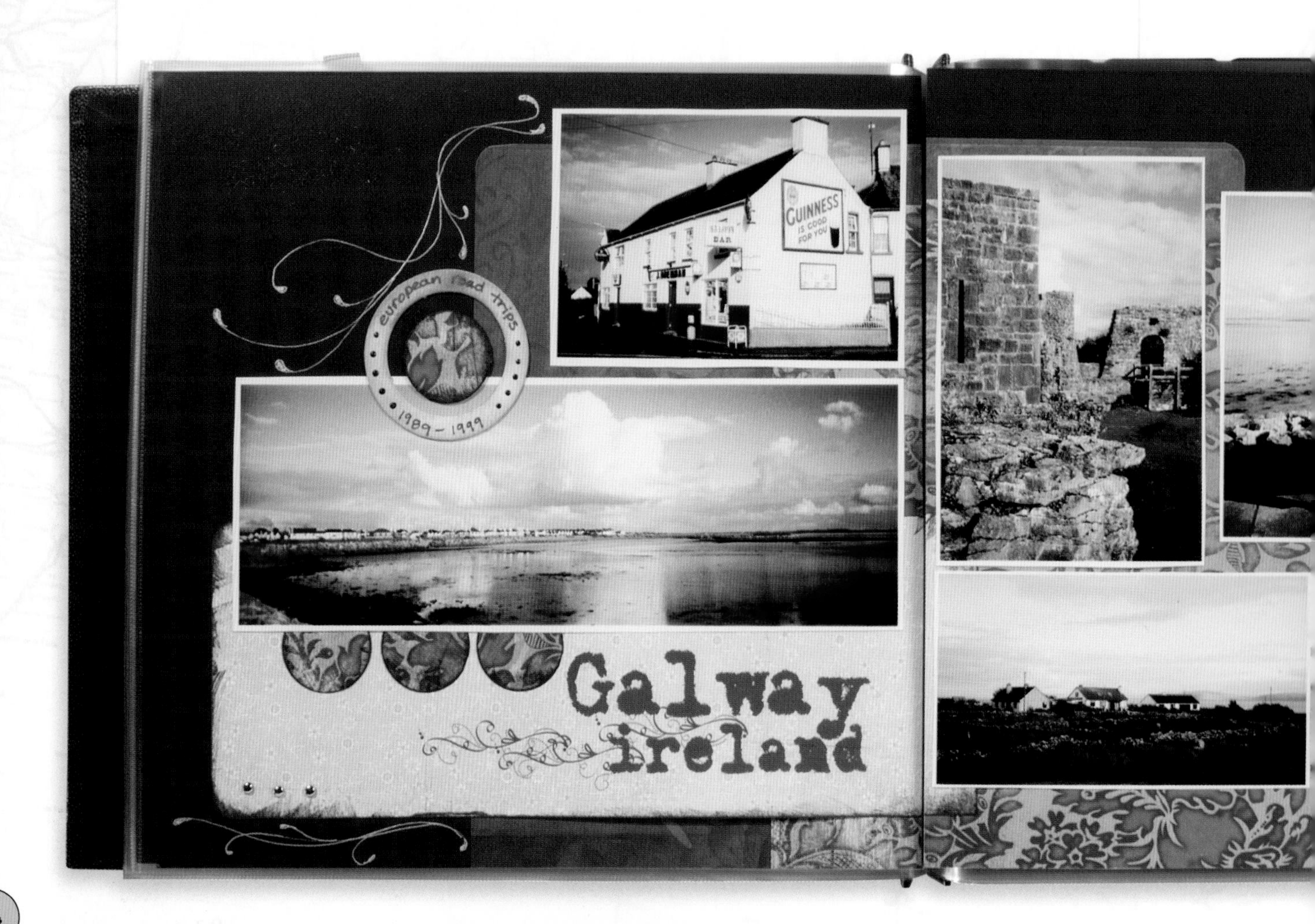

european road trip
1989 – 1995
Copenhagen
denmark
TATOVERING
Barb, Chris Norris
The most expensive
been in.

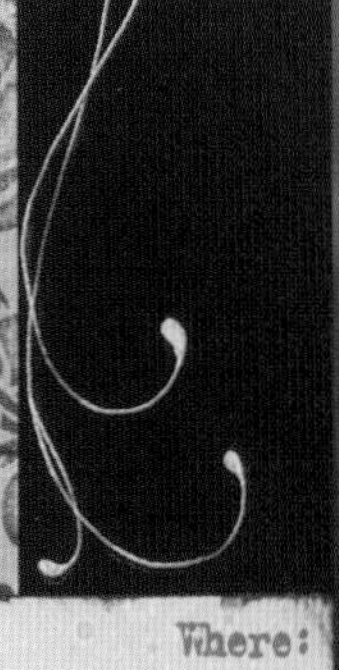

Where:
Galway, Ireland
Who:
Barb and Mom Noland
When:
June 1995
Observations:
Ireland is the greenest place on the planet. The fog and the food is bad, but the people are great!

Venice
italy
Where:
Venice, Italy
Who:
Barb Hogan and Barb Myers
When:
July 1995
Observations:
The light is indescrible . It's beastly hot in July. It's the most romantic city in the world

Road Trip by the Numbers

Linda Harrison of Sarasota, Florida

There's nothing that will fill your heart with more warmth and nostalgia than the classic American road trip. Making an annual trek from Florida to North Carolina is a tradition for Linda's family, but she was in search of a new way to record their two-lane highway adventures. When she stumbled upon a pre-made album in the shape of car, she knew she hit the crafter's jackpot.

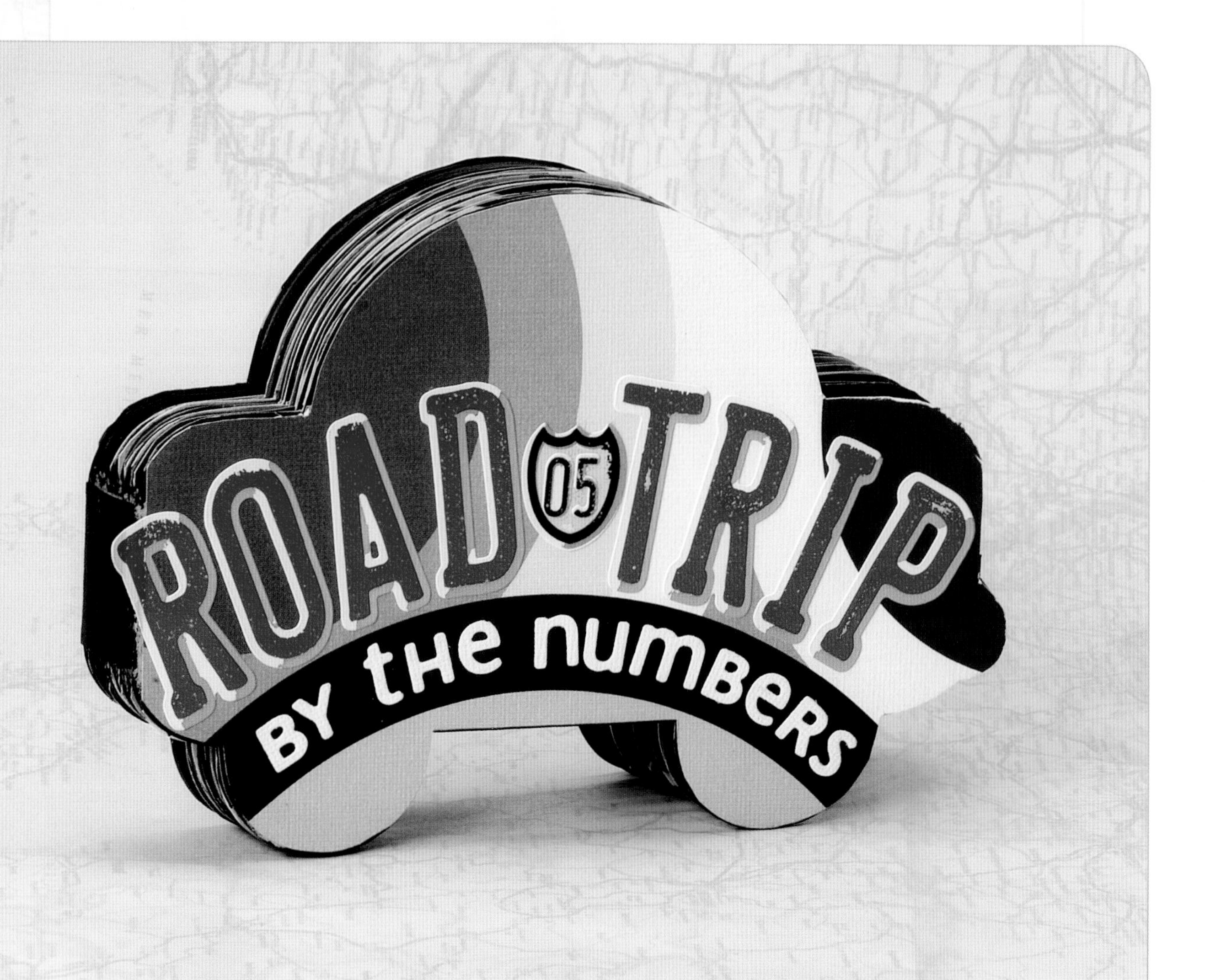

1307
miles driven
FROM SARASOTA, FL TO CASHIERS, NC

To create a project that is simple and fun, select a pre-made album in a unique format, and trim the photos to match the size and shape of the pages. Not only will this add visual interest, it will reflect the theme of your project. A fun way to shake up your journaling is to use numbers to relay interesting facts or statistics such as miles driven or number of bags packed. Along the way, snap photos of everything from the mundane to the sublime, including packing up the car, pumping gas and stopping for snacks. Keep your lettering quick and easy by using die-cut letters or stickers that can be easily adhered to album pages.

The Road Trip Home

Eileen Aber of Cincinnati, Ohio

The beauty and adventure of the open road is captured in this 6.5" x 6" (16.5cm x 15cm) spiral-bound album. From cruising down Highway 1 on California's coast to exploring the rugged desert country of Arizona, Eileen gives her readers a snapshot view of the unique beauty seen on this cross-country journey.

If you've gathered a good collection of photos from different regions, an easy way to bring the whole album together is to use a map in place of patterned paper. Since most road atlases are updated annually, simply find an older version and tear away! A map background will bring a cohesive feel and will also provide the opportunity to highlight trip destinations, as Eileen did in this example with concentric circles and arrows. A great way to set the mood and tone of your album is to include a fitting quote on the opening spread. You can add further imagery by using descriptive word stickers and handwritten journaling. Don't forget to include important stats such as dates, road names and number of miles driven.

As you journey through life, choose your destinations well, but do not hurry there. You will arrive soon enough. And if, upon arrival, you find that your destination is not exactly as you had dreamed, do not be disappointed. Think of all you would have missed, but for the journey there, and know that the true worth of your travels lie not in where you come to be at journey's end, but in who you come to be along the way.
-source unknown
PARADISE
CALIFORNIA
oasis
WATER
postcard from the edge
Surf
sand
BEACH
Our last sunset as California residents
—Laguna Beach 7.31.05
in Dayton Friday night and
night at my parent's. In the
we took off for our new home:
CINCINNATI, OHIO!!
To Ohio
Destination
crossing the ohio border
ACHIEVE (E-CHEV) 1. TO COMPLETE SOME EXPECTATION SUCCESSFULLY 2. TO OBTAIN OR REACH WHAT ONE SET OUT TO DO
we made it!!
2,349 miles

The Bus Diaries

Alecia Grimm of Atlanta, Georgia

Alecia moved far beyond the role of curious tourist during her backpacking trip through Central America. Immersing herself in the culture and people, she journeyed to different locales, gathering a wealth of memorabilia along the way. Among her cache is a collection of bus tickets. Wanting to both preserve these transportation treasures as well as tell her story, she created a handmade 6" x 8" (15cm x 20cm) chipboard album bound with large jump rings and polka-dot ribbon.

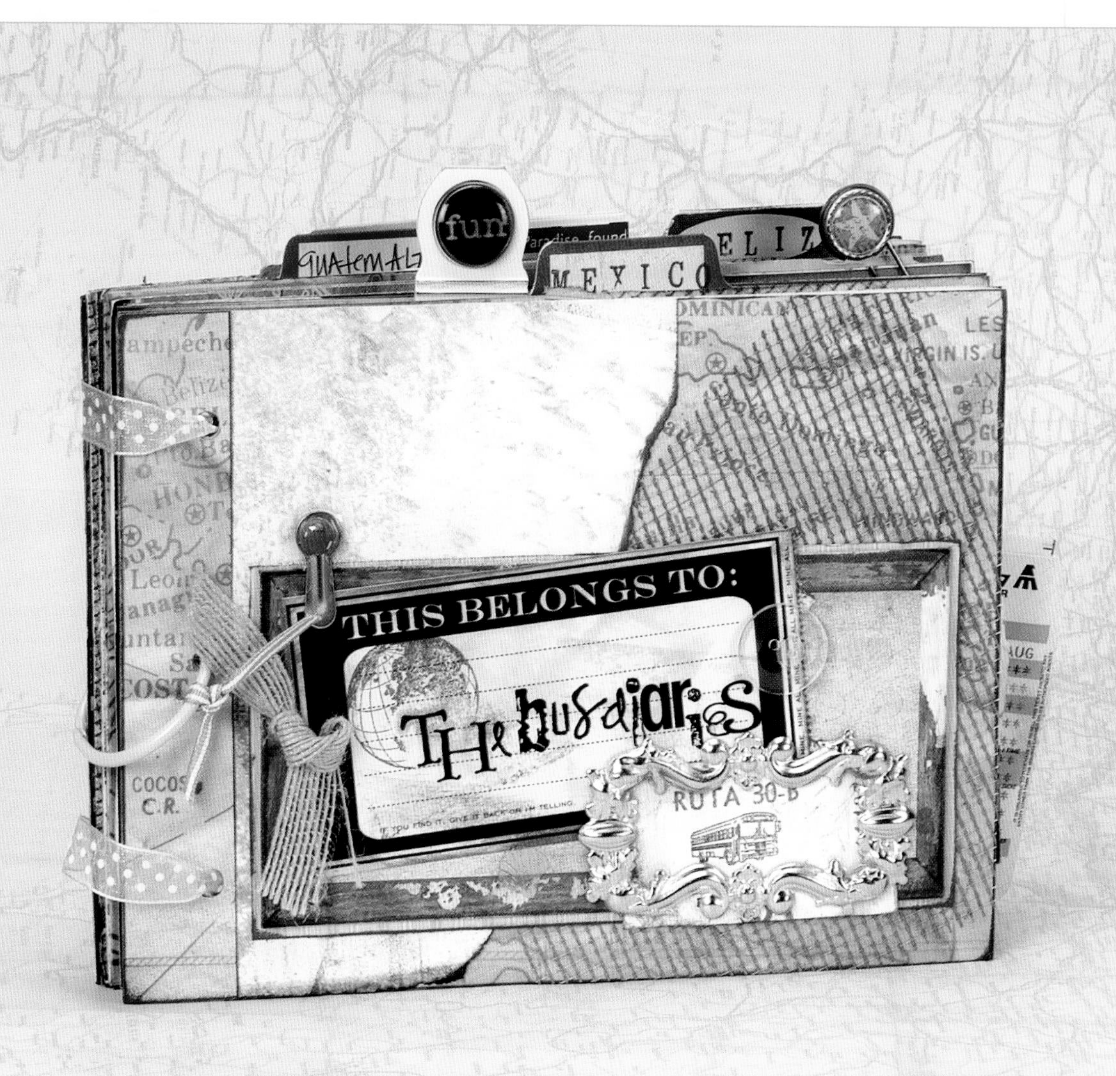

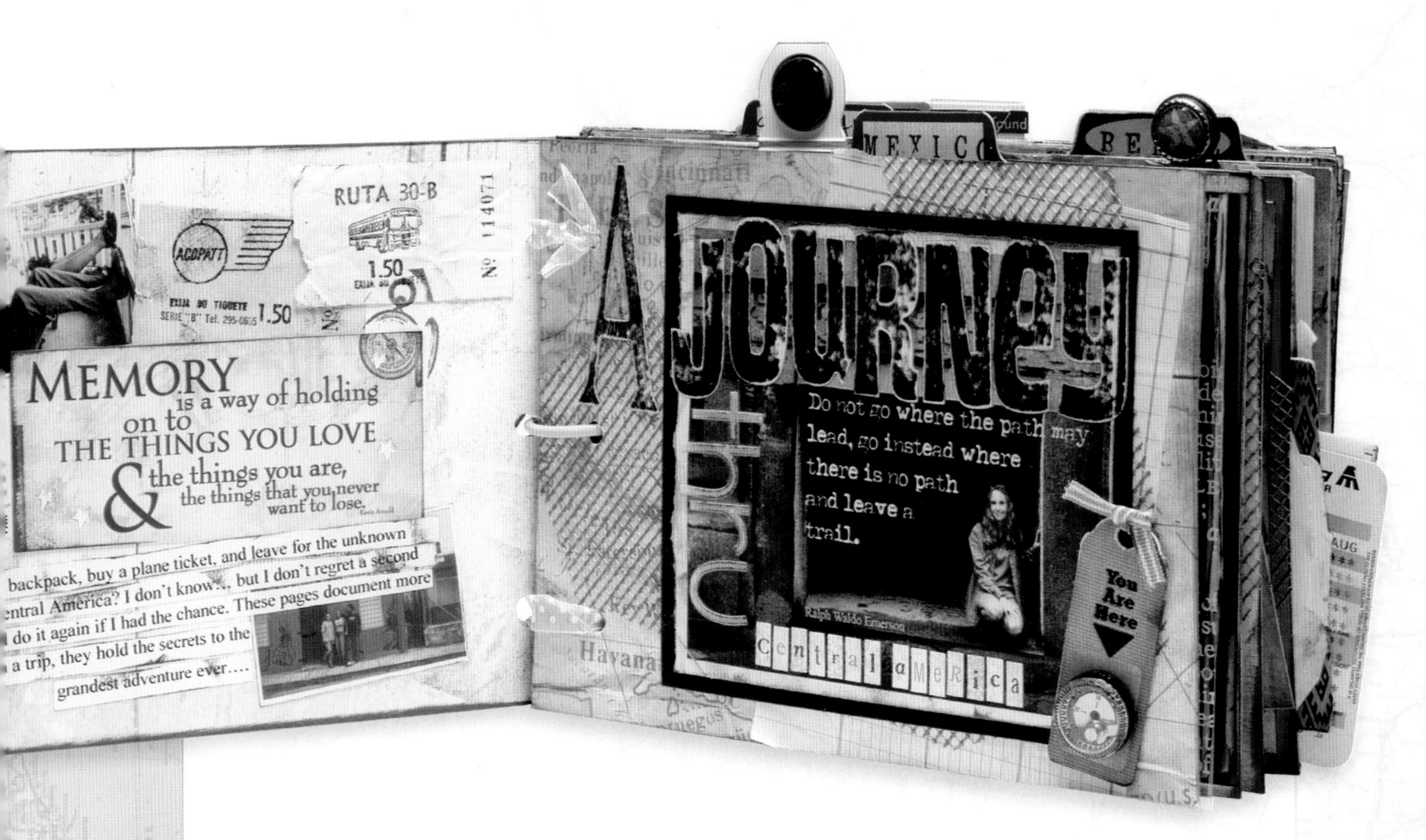

A handy way to both exhibit and store precious memorabilia such as tickets, brochures or maps is to create an accordion-folded stadium display. Simply trim a piece of vellum to fit the dimensions of your album, fold accordion-style and use staples to secure the sides. Another fun album idea is to take a picture of your suitcase or belongings. It will truly burn your travels in your memory, and it's a great way to add a sense of time and place while helping explain what was needed for the trip.

The Bus Diaries

Alecia Grimm of Atlanta, Georgia

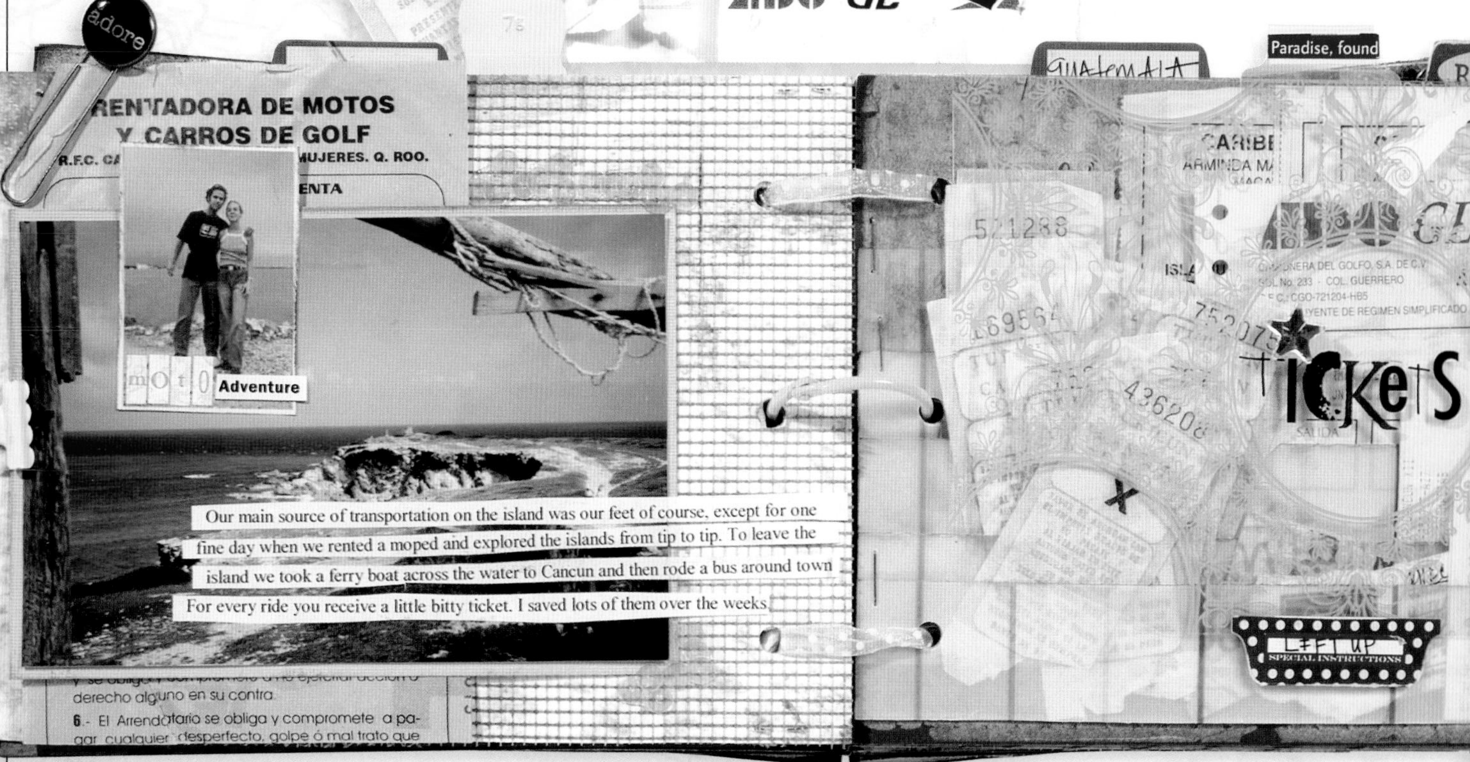

Paradise, found
Here I am at the Youth Hostel in Isla Mujeres. What you see spread around me is my backpack, 2 pairs of shoes, a towel, sunscreen, 2 stacks of clothes, my guide book, tooth brush, shampoo, my camera, a notebook and a few pens. That's it. And below is a photo of my glamorous outdoor bedroom at the hostel. Talk about the simplifying.
under the stars
bliss and pure joy often are found in the simplest of everyday things.
REAL
nature

Memorabilia CHECKLIST

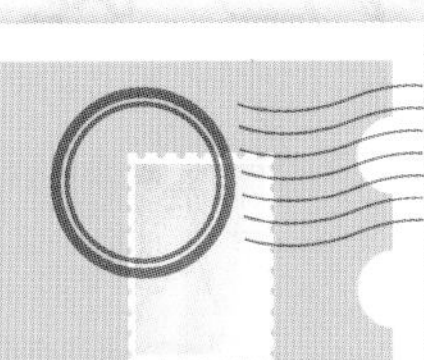

Souvenirs and mementos collected during your travels are worthy of remembrance. These treasured trinkets can help capture a once-in-a lifetime experience or elicit a precious travel memory when housed in a travel album.

- **Tickets**
- **Itinerary**
- **Programs & brochures**
- **Passports**
- **Maps**
- **Foreign currency & postage stamps**
- **Receipts**
- **Matchbooks**
- **Sand, seashells & other beach finds**
- **Postcards**
- **Foreign newspaper clippings**

Chapter two

Savvy IN THE CITY

Are you someone who likes to wonder among skyscraper giants, shop till you drop at busy markets or trendy boutiques, or meander through formal gardens or elegant squares? Do you look for interesting facts and amazing curiosities when walking about town? Street by street, building by building, the great cities of the world offer globetrotters a wealth of tradition and culture to savor. This chapter will delight you with examples of albums that feature trinkets and treasures sharing the sights and sounds of amazing cities. Discover techniques for using color effectively, alternatives to the typical album format, journaling tips and ways to weave a thread of continuity through a variety of photographs. Rich in history, infused with vibrant architecture, and bustling with style, energy and attitude, cities mesmerize us with their splendor. Take a walk down the sidewalks of these great meccas, and you're sure to find a wealth of ideas for city scrapbooks.

OUR
trip
to
NIAGARA
FALLS
the SIGHTS
12.00
CLIFTON HILL
FUN BY THE FALLS
HWY. 420
CANADA
TOP OF CLIFTON HILL,
ONTARIO, CANADA

London Expedition

Diana Lyn McGraw of Virginia Beach, Virginia

London is a city of shadows and light. Camera-toting crowds flock to its streets to capture its history and architecture. Diana journeyed to the awe-inspiring city and came back with photos no less than stellar. Polished pages set atop clean white cardstock come together in this 11" x 7.5" (28cm x 19cm) album.

Keep your album simple by focusing on the photos. Color-blocking is an effective technique to use in combination with a monochromatic color scheme. Employing this technique will help the photos pop right off the page. Use white space to add handwritten journaling and decorative design elements while keeping the spread balanced. Add paper flowers, chipboard letters and stamped scrolls for a final touch of grace and formality.

Dad you took me on my first trip to London and it was
absolutely amazing - one of the best experiences of my life.
first class
the whole trip. I felt like royalty. I love London.
LONDON
Our hotel, the Langham Hilton, one of the most prestigious hotels in the city London.
Everyone drinks tea at tea time
every night we would socialize in the lounge with a few drinks. Champagne is my new favorite drink.
the experience
AMAZING
Apparently in London, when you go to the clubs you have to be on the list or stand in line. Our concierge not only got us on the list... he got us on the VIP list!
London
L
journey
London
I learned not to wear heels on cobblestone.
vacation
People love McD's portions smaller

I Heart NY

Becky Fleck of Columbus, Montana

Becky resides in Montana, but for one week she was happy to trade Rocky Mountain summits for New York City skyscrapers. Times Square, Broadway musicals, crowded streets and ethnic foods all enticed her with their big city charm. But a standard flip-the-page album would not do justice to such an amazing trip. So Becky put on her creative thinking cap, and this out-of-the-box masterpiece was born.

Becky used a scroll saw to create the wooden letters and pedestal, but an alternative is to purchase pre-made wooden letters at a craft or home decor store and then decorate them as desired. To include the heart-shaped album pages, simply drill two holes through the wooden heart (or shape of your choosing) to fit jumbo jump rings that will hold the pages. Don't forget photos, journaling and any accents or designs that add your own personal touch.

I had such a great time on my trip to new York in May 2006! Ames gave me an amazing grand tour of everything—Manhattan, the Bronx, the gorgeous countryside where she lives, several local nurseries, the famous Stew Leonard's, and a fabulous Broadway play topped it off. It was a terrific five-day trip!
Walking from Grand Central Station up Broadway was so cool. There were tons of street vendors, musicians, coffee shops, bakeries, stores, hotels, and more restaurants than I could count. The sidewalks were filled with people and I quickly discovered that if you didn't keep up the pace, you got bumped into or ran over!
I love Ames!
I love Times Square!
MAMMA MIA!
Seattle Cafe

Cities of Europe

Linda Harrison of Sarasota, Florida

The cities of Europe have for centuries been the favorite subjects of painters and photographers. Now it's a favorite for scrap-happy artists as well. Linda wanted to feature the collection of photos from her 1989 trip, but in a stylish and fresh way. She breathes new life into her pictures of each European metropolis by decorating the album in charming simplicity.

If you're looking to show various destinations in a single album, a repeated cardstock base will keep it cohesive. A handy way to call out each city is to use circular monograms atop patterned paper. Add a bit of texture with paper flowers constructed of petals, sequins and ribbon. Include all the important trip details in computer-printed journaling displayed in a contemporary font.

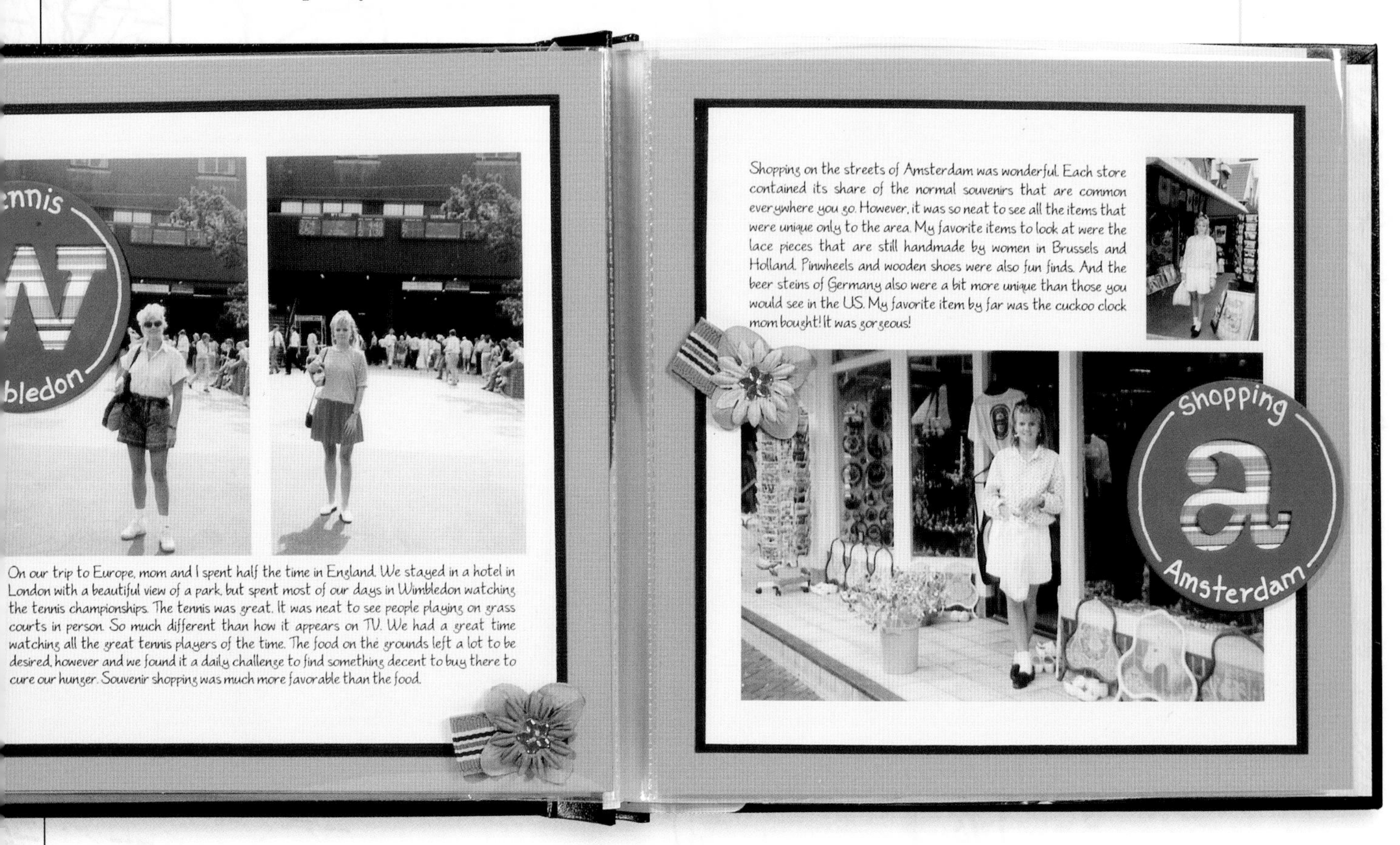

W
On our trip to Europe, mom and I spent half the time in England. We stayed in a hotel in London with a beautiful view of a park, but spent most of our days in Wimbledon watching the tennis championships. The tennis was great. It was neat to see people playing on grass courts in person. So much different than how it appears on TV. We had a great time watching all the great tennis players of the time. The food on the grounds left a lot to be desired, however and we found it a daily challenge to find something decent to buy there to cure our hunger. Souvenir shopping was much more favorable than the food.
Shopping on the streets of Amsterdam was wonderful. Each store contained its share of the normal souvenirs that are common everywhere you go. However, it was so neat to see all the items that were unique only to the area. My favorite items to look at were the lace pieces that are still handmade by women in Brussels and Holland. Pinwheels and wooden shoes were also fun finds. And the beer steins of Germany also were a bit more unique than those you would see in the US. My favorite item by far was the cuckoo clock mom bought! It was gorgeous!
Shopping
a
Amsterdam

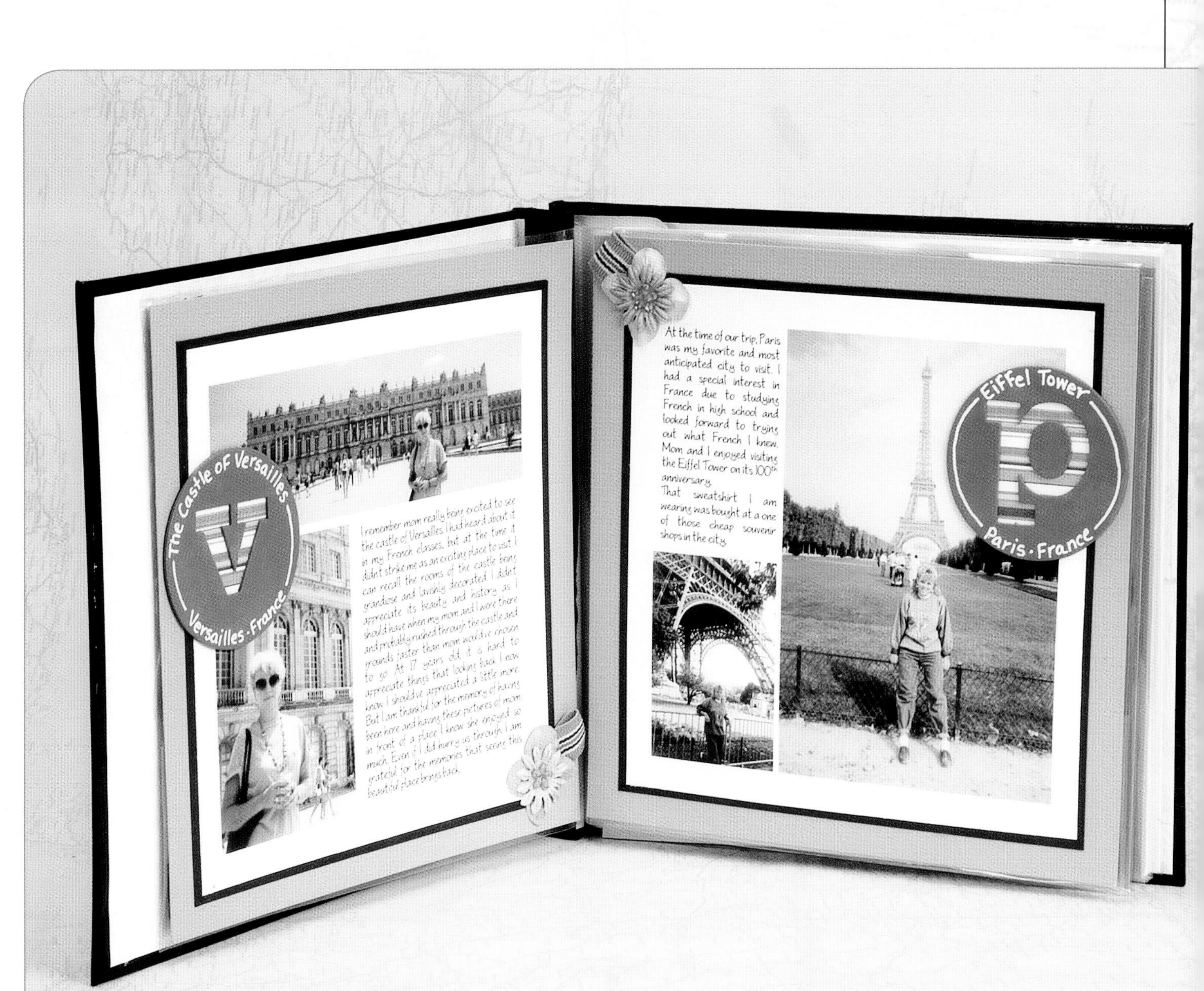
The Castle of Versailles
Versailles · France
I remember mom really being excited to see
the castle of Versalles. I had heard about it
in my French classes, but at the time it
didn't strike me as an exciting place to visit. I
can recall the rooms of the castle being
grandiose and lavishly decorated. I didn't
appreciate its beauty and history as I
should have when my mom and I were there
and probably rushed through the castle and
grounds faster than mom would've chosen
to go. At 17 years old, it is hard to
appreciate things that looking back I now
know I should've appreciated a little more.
But I am thankful for the memory of having
been here and having these pictures of mom
in front of a place I know she enjoyed so
much. Even if I did hurry us through, I am
grateful for the memories that seeing this
beautiful place brings back.
At the time of our trip, Paris
was my favorite and most
anticipated city to visit. I
had a special interest in
France due to studying
French in high school and
looked forward to trying
out what French I knew.
Mom and I enjoyed visiting
the Eiffel Tower on its 100th
anniversary.
That sweatshirt I am
wearing was bought at a one
of those cheap souvenir
shops in the city.
Eiffel Tower
Paris · France

Our Trip to Niagara Falls

Vicki Boutin of Burlington, Ontario, Canada

The roaring falls of Niagara drew Vicki's family to this magical place for a camping trip. Enchanted by the sights and sounds of both nature and the variety of fun activities, she created this two-ring binder chipboard album accented with patterned paper and a collection of mini photos for a fun and playful look.

For a cool and easy way to add some fun, attach clippings of tourist brochures or miniature souvenirs such as this toy camera viewfinder. Key chains can also be put to creative use as Vicki shows on the cover of this album. She simply removed the ring from the "Niagara Falls" plastic letter key chain, and adhered the letters to her cover as part of the title. Mini bottle caps enhanced with rub-on letters, plastic lettering, labels and epoxy stickers also work as unique type treatments.

What a beautiful day! This street is
just CRAZY!! Where else can
you go & see such a scene?
BURGER KING
Clifton Hill
The Street of fun at the Falls
OFFICIAL OFFICIAL
100% SMILES
OFFICIAL OFFICIAL
BRICK CITY
Created with LEGO Bricks
We walked the hills and
tried to take it all in. CRAZY!
Clifton hill

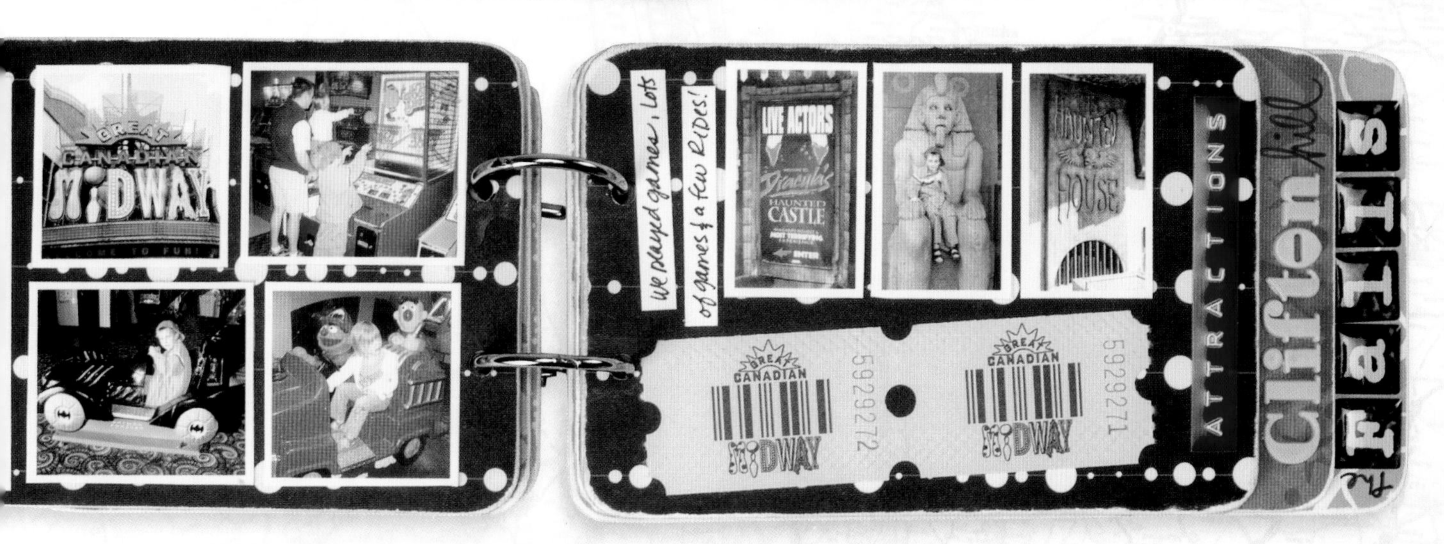

GREAT CANADIAN MIDWAY
We played games, lots
of games & a few RIDES!
LIVE ACTORS
Dracula's HAUNTED CASTLE
HAUNTED HOUSE
GREAT CANADIAN MIDWAY
5929272
GREAT CANADIAN MIDWAY
5929271
ATTRACTIONS
Clifton hill
The FALLS

a daytrip to the
Falls to see the Sights
There is so much to see
in Niagara Falls!! Wow!
the SIGHTS
Times
FUN
ATTRACTIONS
Clifton hill
The FALLS

Washington, D.C.

Caroline Ikeji of Alhambra, California

Boasting some of our country's most celebrated symbols of patriotism, the sights and sounds of Washington, D.C., are some of the most fun to explore. But what if you come home to find your pictures aren't what you expected? Albums heavy with journaling are a great alternative! Caroline says, "I came home with a well-kept journal, but not many great photos. So I decided to create a travel journal with photos and memorabilia sprinkled throughout to accent my text." It worked perfectly.

Have fun combining a delicious mix of pattern papers to represent your theme. An easy way to document your itinerary is to assign each day a spread and use circular tabs to number accordingly. Type your journaling in a small but readable font to share all the important travel details.

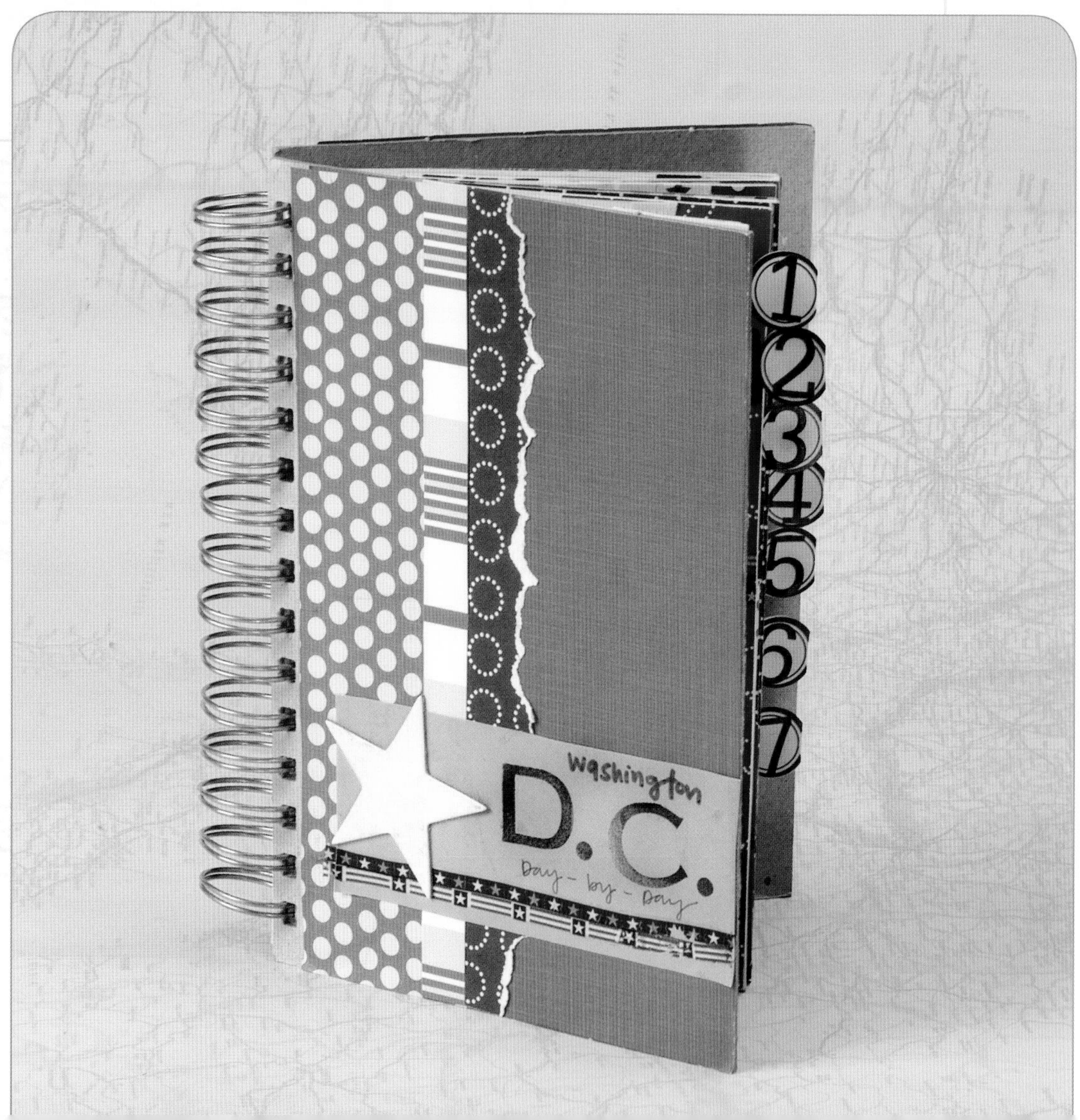

Tour of the
United States Capitol
Washington, D.C.
Conducted by the Capitol Guide Service
Photography is prohibited in the third floor Congressional Galleries

Today, almost everywhere we went had tight security. It felt like we were in the airport again! They would X-ray or look through our bags and make us walk through metal detectors.

We took the Metro today. Lynn kind of made us nervous, because we had to rush so they wouldn't close the doors before everyone got in. Since it was rush hour, it was pretty crowded and we couldn't get into one car, but about two stations we got off, there were a lot of empty seats to we got to sit down. We went from Foggy Bottom-GWU to Capitol South.

When we got off, we went to the Supreme Court for breakfast. Pretty much all we did was eat in the cafeteria, so we didn't see much of anything else.

After the Supreme Court, we went to the U.S. Capitol. The guide there kept telling personal stories about working there and kept cracking jokes, so we didn't learn too much from him. We learned that in the House and Senate chambers, there are two statues of historic people from each state.

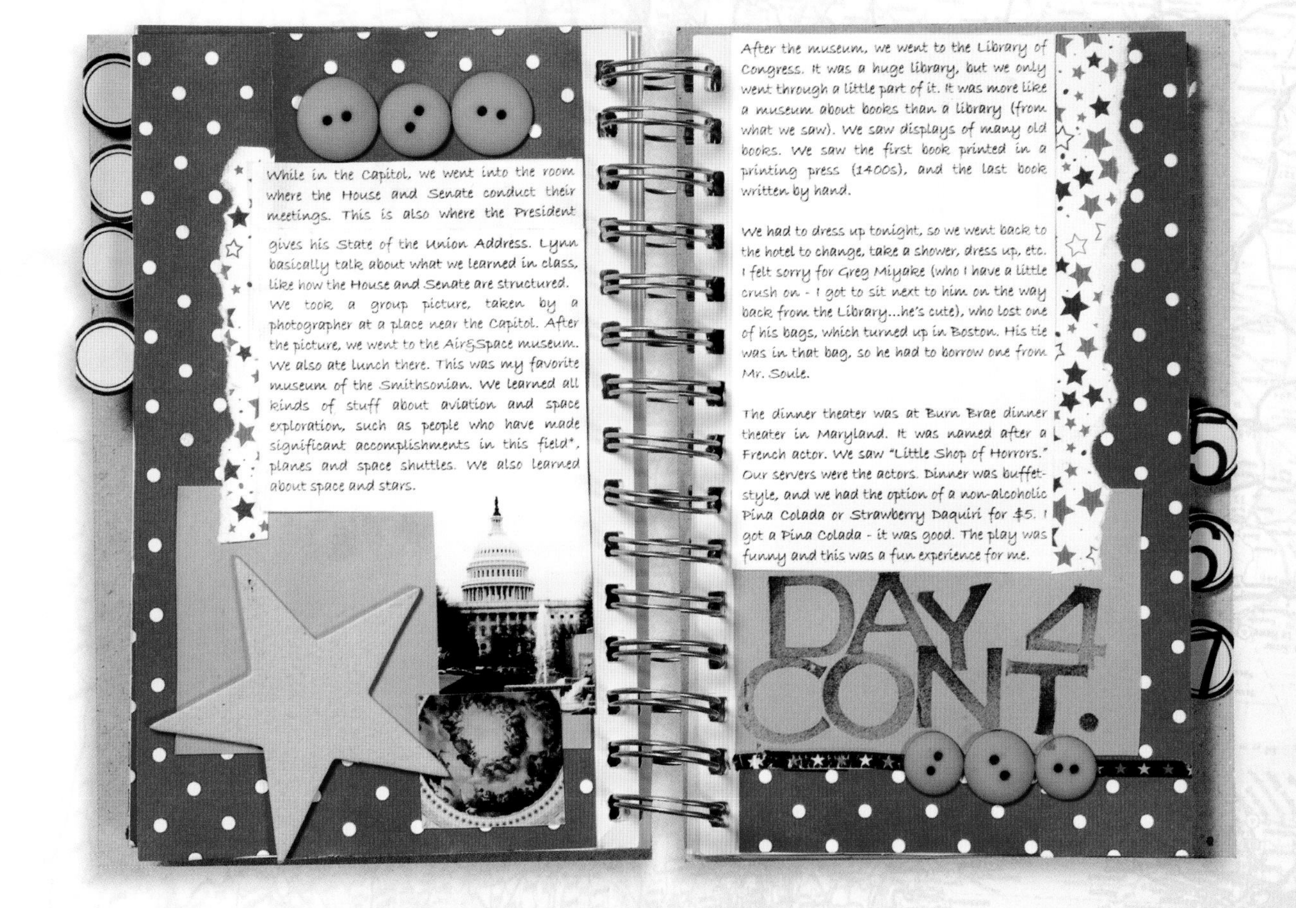

While in the Capitol, we went into the room where the House and Senate conduct their meetings. This is also where the President gives his State of the Union Address. Lynn basically talk about what we learned in class, like how the House and Senate are structured. We took a group picture, taken by a photographer at a place near the Capitol. After the picture, we went to the Air&Space museum. We also ate lunch there. This was my favorite museum of the Smithsonian. We learned all kinds of stuff about aviation and space exploration, such as people who have made significant accomplishments in this field*, planes and space shuttles. We also learned about space and stars.
After the museum, we went to the Library of Congress. It was a huge library, but we only went through a little part of it. It was more like a museum about books than a library (from what we saw). We saw displays of many old books. We saw the first book printed in a printing press (1400s), and the last book written by hand.
We had to dress up tonight, so we went back to the hotel to change, take a shower, dress up, etc. I felt sorry for Greg Miyake (who I have a little crush on - I got to sit next to him on the way back from the Library...he's cute), who lost one of his bags, which turned up in Boston. His tie was in that bag, so he had to borrow one from Mr. Soule.
The dinner theater was at Burn Brae dinner theater in Maryland. It was named after a French actor. We saw "Little Shop of Horrors." Our servers were the actors. Dinner was buffet-style, and we had the option of a non-alcoholic Pina Colada or Strawberry Daquiri for $5. I got a Pina Colada - it was good. The play was funny and this was a fun experience for me.
DAY 4
CONT.
5
6
7

My Favorite Cities

May Flaum of Vacaville, California

Whether she's attending a Red Sox game at Fenway Park or walking through a historic neighborhood in downtown Savannah, May can't get enough of her favorite cities. So in true scrapbooking spirit, she decided to create a post-bound album with pages dedicated to each one. Even though each spread features different colors, pattern and textures, she wanted to keep a cohesive feel throughout by using the city names as titles and typing all her journaling in a clean style.

For a fun background paper, crop a map to fit over your page. You can add different type treatments in various fonts to complement the look. If you're lacking memorabilia, use a few decorative design elements such as rub-on flourishes or silk flowers to dress up the page. An easy way to add detailed information is to include an article, newspaper clipping or brochure highlighting your favorite city.

boston
BOSTON RED SOX
FENWAY PARK
BOSTON
I'll admit it. I am in love with Boston. My first visit was due to illness (my sister was at Boston Medical) but I still knew that this was a place that I was meant to visit. Yes, each time I visit this city I find myself in either freezing cold and pouring rain, or blistering heat. Why is that? I don't know, but even with my bad luck with weather I still am in love with Boston.
I love Boston
Fenway
Yes, it was pouring rain when I got to visit, but it was amazing never the less. I'm still not a huge baseball fan, but the tour allowed us to see the park inside and out, and get a better appreciation for just how special it is.
One of my favorite places on earth is Boston Common and the public gardens. I love seeing the children playing games, all of the lush green plants, and the ducks swimming in the pond. I also love that when you exit you'll find yourself surrounded by posh hotels, fantastic restaurants, and world class shopping.
Finale is truly heaven on earth. This restaurant specializes in desserts that are more amazing, and more delicious than you could ever imagine. A trip to Boston is not complete until I taste one of their signature desserts like crème brule or one of their chocolate trios.
Finale
I will never forget the day my mother and I went sightseeing all around the city. One of the highlights was our stop at the Boston Tea Party museum. In addition to learning a lot we got to have iced tea, and throw some bushels of tea overboard!
Tea Party
The map on this page is the one I used on my last trip to Boston to help me get around the city. We always walked and utilized the T (subway system) when in town, and that added to the fun of our experiences. I am sure that each time I visit "bean town" I'll continue to add new memories, new favorites, and take even more photos of this city that forever has a cherished place in my heart.

2 Travel

Suzy Plantamura of Laguna Niguel, California

Coursing with energy, Vancouver is the getaway of getaways. A favorite stop en route to a ski resort in British Columbia, Suzy and her family take time on their journey to explore this amazing city. Wanting to create a spiral-bound album that would also serve as a useful travel guide, Suzy displayed a variety of panoramic shots capturing beautiful cityscapes.

For a quick and easy way to create a cover, simply use a pre-made metal plate resembling a license plate. Mix up your selection of photos by including both color and black-and-white. If your photos are in need of cleaning up, photo-editing software to the rescue! Feature destinations and attractions that are close to your heart. In this example, Suzy chose to display her favorite haunts—a local food market, a well-traveled street and a Chinese bistro. For lettering, handwritten journaling, die-cut letters, stickers and rub-ons pleasantly combine to tell her story. Add dashes of ribbon and stamped designs for the finishing touches.

2 Travel

Suzy Plantamura of Laguna Niguel, California

We love going to Granville Market for produce, cheese, salami and breads.
GRANVILLE MARKET
We alway stop by before heading to whistler.
MEMORIES
explore
GRANVILLE ISLAND
emilycarr
We love the kids market and shops!
Great shopping, food and fun for everyone!

EXPLORING my favorite CITY...
A Visitors Guide to the Best Places to explore!
VANCOUVER
Canada
Restaurants
Exploring
Recreation
Lodging
MEMORIES

Insider's GUIDE

Strong images and evocative descriptions can make an ordinary travel album extraordinary. But in the frenzy of travel preparation, it is easy to forget essential items that will aid in your documentation. Consider bringing these basics before hitting the road.

- **Camera, film, batteries, owner's manual, extra memory card, and any ancillary equipment such as a tripod or lenses**
- **Notebook, pen and/or laptop for journaling on the road**
- **Memorabilia storage such as plastic envelopes or manila folders**

Chapter three

Life's a Beach

Is your vision of paradise being cooled by a tropical breeze while listening to the steady steam-rolled surf lapping onto strands of soft sand? Perhaps you seek more enthralling escapades such as hiking to jagged volcanic cliffs or snorkeling in coral sea waters. Whether you go for a laid-back vibe or dive into adventure, a sun-filled getaway is solitude for the soul. And even though you can't bring paradise home, you can inject a taste of it into your albums. In the pages that follow, you'll find albums of every variety—handmade, gatefold, postcard and more—each illustrating the magic and beauty of sandy shores. Discover a few new journaling techniques, find ways to display a wealth of postcards, and learn how to fashion albums in interesting and unusual formats. So put on your flip-flops, turn on some ukulele music and peruse the magnificent examples that follow.

go
The very 1st thing we do is go to Joe's and get fresh fruit + to Barneys for groceries.
This is the view from the cottage window— you can hear the waves + the view is soothing + gorgeous.
mich igan
at the cottage
SANTAREN CHANNEL

Cape Hatteras

Courtney Walsh of Winnebago, Illinois

Cradled on the waves of the Atlantic, the stretches of beach and sand dunes on Cape Hatteras offer a retreat for the soul. To keep the trip forever in her memory, Courtney created a handmade three-ring album in a rich complementary color scheme composed of cool blue and warm orange.

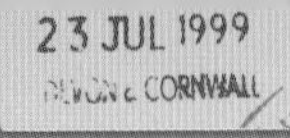

To create an album that is truly your own, trim cardstock and patterned paper into 8.5" x 11" (21cm x 28cm) pages, punch holes and weave ribbon to bind. If you have photos, brochures or postcards you want to be accessible but not part of the basic design, create a pocket to safely tuck them in. Courtney played hers up with a scalloped edge and colorful buttons. If you have a three-dimensional item you'd like to include, like the rock in Courtney's album, trim a piece of transparent packaging and stitch it to your page. This innovative idea is both functional and attractive.

Moments 2 Remember

Diana Lyn McGraw of Virginia Beach, Virginia

One of the reasons we scrapbook is to record the memories we want to remember for the rest of our lives. The night before Diana's husband was deployed, the family gathered at their favorite beach for a photo shoot. The experience held special meaning, so she celebrated its significance in this 7" x 10" (18cm x 25cm) gatefold album.

If you want to focus on telling your story, use hidden journaling techniques such as envelopes, pockets and tags. The gatefold format is unique because it lends additional real estate and dimension to add these smaller interactive elements. For this spread Diana wanted the photos to tell the story of the their family. So instead of adding blocks of clunky text, she kept her journaling to a minimum and allowed the evocative images to take center stage. For the short phrases she did include, she used a variety of type treatments to keep the tone warm and inviting.

For additional visual interest, take a series of action photos to create a mini photomontage or place a pre-printed transparency in a tilted position over a photo to make it pop off the page. Paper flowers dotted over floral, striped and polka-dot paper are the perfect design elements to add an extra punch of color as well as texture. Ink the edges of paper blocks with brown ink to add a distressed feeling and to provide a uniform, eye-pleasing appearance.

Hawaii Postcard Album

Caroline Ikeji of Alhambra, California

Whether you're hiking the rim of a volcano or diving into pristine turquoise waters in search of an aquatic wonderland, a trip to Hawaii will fill you with the spirit of aloha. Bring some of that spirit home and infuse it into an adorable postcard album. Caroline collected a multitude of postcards on her trip, but feared they would end up collecting dust in a box in her closet. So she got creative and decided to organize them in an inexpensive post-bound picture album. To keep it fun, she added a playful mix tropical papers and accents.

A postcard album is a great way to construct a quick album that's quick and easy. Because the handwritten correspondence from the back of the postcards will be covered, remember to include important journaling details and select a type treatment that reflects your theme. A rainbow of patterned papers and silk flowers will brightly bloom next to stunning photos. Add buttons, ribbon, glitter or brads for decorative touches.

Pensacola Beach

Michelle Van Etten of Pensacola, Florida

Michelle and her family escaped to the sun-kissed beaches of Pensacola where the sand is as soft as baby's bottom. With her new digital camera in hand, she snapped an array of pictures of her own baby playfully dancing in gentle tides. These great photos called for a great display, and this circular chipboard album worked perfectly.

Trim patterned papers to cover the chipboard circles and adhere a few glossy accents to add some shine. A great way to include more pictures but still tell your story is to add journaling to tags. Keep it playful by adding descriptive words that emphasize the mood or feeling of the event. A soufflé pen is a handy tool for outlining letters to give them that extra punch of color. Accent with ribbons, fiber and paper flowers for texture and dimension.

2 if by Sea

Becky Fleck of Columbus, Montana

New Zealand boasts exquisite beaches and a gently rolling landscape. On a quest for some coastal adventures, Becky and her husband took their time savoring everything the serene paradise had to offer. Coming home with myriad photos, she knew the perfect way to remember the trip would be in a circular chipboard album.

If the circle shape suits you, use a circle cutting system to quickly and easily crop your photos. Add type treatments over photos using image-editing software or select a mood-appropriate font and print onto cardstock. If you're looking for an easy way to journal, try the list format. In this example, Becky recorded what she remembered about each place they visited on their journey. Her lists included scenery, activities they took part in, even sensory details such as smell and taste. This is a great way to relay the small but important details.

good times
what i remember:
gravel beaches
starfish on the beach
hot coffee on the beach
sunshine
flocks of seagulls
dolomite point at punakaiki
hole in the rock at cathedral cove
loud,
beachwood
hermit crabs
ocean spray
the coastal adventures of two mountain dwellers
haast south island to cathedral cove north island
new zealand
march 3-8 2006
you and me

Our Faves and Memories

Linda Harrison of Sarasota, Florida

A lush tropical island getaway with several hundred miles of coral reef, the Turks and Caicos are blessed with beaches that make you say "ah." Linda recorded her family's unforgettable vacation in this mini chipboard tag book dressed in tropical colors to reflect the fun and carefree feeling they experienced.

Try a "he said, she said" approach to journaling if you're looking for a new way to record thoughts and impressions as well as add in someone else's point of view. Topics or categories can include favorite photos, unexpected roles or favorite treats—anything you found memorable or out of the ordinary. If you want to mix up your type treatments, die-cut letters are a great choice because they are quick and easy and allow you to mix colors and patterns. To add a decorative touch and further enhance your theme, include fanciful ribbons or a repeating die-cut such as this tropical flower.

unexpected
role
Rob says :
I was definitely the official cart-pusher of the trip. It was fine because it really helped us get around the Island. It was Robby's favorite way to travel and it helped to hold our stuff too.
Linda says :
On this vacation, it was nice to come back with some photos that showed I was there! I had an unexpected role IN FRONT of the camera this trip
Preferred
Rob says :
I really enjoyed sitting and sharing a refreshment with my little man. Robby liked having milk and I liked the 'Island' milk. It was a nice break from all the Island activities.
Linda says :
My favorite Island treat was definitely when the poolside grill was fired up for the day. I enjoyed those bar-b-que lunches by the water most.

Michigan Travel Box

Hanni Baumgartner of Warsaw, Indiana

Hanni's album on her family's annual trip to the cabin on Lake Michigan resonates with nostalgia, warmth and retro flair. Wanting to record their family's summer tradition in a fun and unique way, she created a mini box album that's large enough for album pages, seashells and heartwarming family memories that will be cherished for a lifetime. She even included a dash of sand for good measure.

To create a mini box album like Hanni's, select a small cardboard box, paint the exterior and add a thin layer of decoupage medium to prevent chips and cracks. Select colors and embellishments that will coordinate with your album pages and will reinforce your theme. In this example, felt, grosgrain ribbon, a paper flower and a button all gracefully adorn the box's cover while supporting the happy beach theme.

This is the view
from the cottage
window—you
can hear the waves
+ the view is
soothing + gorgeous.

Michigan Travel Box

Hanni Baumgartner of Warsaw, Indiana

Red Arrow
02
Sea WitcH
*BeaCh
We're at the beach everyday unless it rains → then it's outlet mall day. There is a private beach at the cottage... we drag our stuff down the old stone steps + the beach is all ours. Jesse + I usually goof around in the water; we go for walks, skip stones, laugh at Jovan's stories, read under the umbrella + drink sweet tea.

Creating the interior pages offers a wealth of creative possibilities. Simply trim cardstock to fit into the size and shape of the cardboard box. Have fun mixing it up by trimming some pages with a straight edge and other with a scalloped edge. Dress up each page with photos and accents. Include photos of smiling faces, signs and logos, and gorgeous natural wonders. To add even a bit more charm, embellish memorabilia with ribbons, buttons or flowers.

Photo OPPORTUNITIES

Most people take a camera on vacation to record what is often a once in a lifetime experience. But if you're a scrapbooker you have another motive—capturing gorgeous shots to display in your albums. Scenes can range from a sunny beach to a spectacular mountain view. Here are some ideas of things and places to snap while en route to your travel paradise.

- **Churches and cathedrals**
- **Parks and gardens**
- **Castles**
- **People and places**
- **Rural life**
- **Wildlife**
- **Art**
- **Snow and ice**
- **Sand and surf**
- **Sunsets**
- **Weather**
- **Skylines**
- **Architecture**
- **Night lights**

Fire Fly
RESORT
05
One year we stayed at
The Firefly instead of the cottage... so cute
but tiny! We met Cocoa (that fiend!)
that summer, and Napoleon Dynamite.

Chapter four

A Natural attraction

Are you a nature junkie? Many of us long for the moments of exploration and adventure when in the unspoiled open space of the great outdoors. Nature's landscape offers a wealth of beauty to document in our scrapbooks, so don't hold back on showing off that postcard-caliber shot of that pristine mountain top or perfect sunset. With the amazing examples featured on the following pages, you'll discover unique album formats such as storybooks and desk calendars, fresh approaches for showcasing older photos, techniques for including memorabilia and valuable photography tips. So whether you like to hike the hidden heart of a virgin woodland, paddle the rapids of a winding river or uncover your own secret corner of the earth, there's a multitude of outdoor adventures just waiting to be featured front and center in your albums.

going
SNOWBALL FIGHT
LET IT SNOW!
our first real snow!
COOL

Have Fly Rod, Will Travel

Becky Fleck of Columbus, Montana

Becky knew a standard mini album wouldn't be large enough to hold all the memories and details of her and her husband's trip to the shores of New Zealand. She says, "We took our laptop with us and made a point of journaling every night. It got a bit tedious by the end, but after we got home I was amazed at how much I had forgotten about the trip until I reread the journal." Instead of leaving all her words on a hard drive, she got creative and turned her story into a handmade storybook complete with chapters, photos and captions.

There are several ways to approach a handmade book. You can create pages using a word-processing or desktop publishing program. You can add photos directly into the design, or crop them traditionally and adhere them to the printed pages. Becky bound her book by hand using a technique called Japanese stab binding, a traditional technique based on 4-hole stitching. This book style will allow you to include as many details as you desire. Don't forget to include random musings, first impressions or parting thoughts.

chicken for our kitchen in one of the gift shops and we bought some homemade apricot and mango chutney. We also located a small pharmacy and I was able to get some much-needed cold medicine. We continued on towards Twizel, stopping for various scenery photos along the way.

Church of the Good Shepherd

Our next stop was a famous old church on Lake Tekapo called The Church of the Good Shepherd. It is situated on a small butte looking over a glorious lake of sapphire blue. The church was built of stone in 1935 as a monument to the settlers of the MacKenzie Valley. Adjacent to the church was a bronze statue of a Border Collie and the 1968 inscription below it reads: "This monument was erected by the runholders of the MacKenzie County and those who also appreciate the value of the collie dog, without the help of which the grazing of this mountain country would be impossible." We arrived in tandem with a bus load of young boys who happened to be from the New Zealand Boys Choir. We both immediately thought of Paul.

Border Collie dedic...

Southern Alps

As we continued on towards Twizel, we drove out of the flatter terrain into a more timbered area. Around a final bend, we were greeted with the magnificent Southern Alps and Lake Pukaki. Although Montana has mountains just as high, this particular range starts at 600 feet and rises up to more than 12,000. It's difficult to take a photo that can adequately convey the enormity of this range.

We arrived in Twizel at 3:30pm, found the Heartland Lodge, and were greeted by the host, Kerry the moment we got out of our car. She showed us around the lodge and then to our room. It was a corner suite upstairs with a view of Mt. Cook and a Koi pond and beautiful gardens directly below the window. Ruby (a black lab) was the resident dog, along with three cats (Frick, Frack and Baby). In no time, I had made friends with all four of them. After we got settled, one of the staff members, Linleigh, suggested we drive up to the Mt. Cook Summit for a nature hike and dinner. She made reservations for us at the Mountaineer Café, so we got cleaned up and headed for Mt. Cook.

the view fron

When we arrived at the visitor's center at 5:00pm, it was just closing so we weren't able to obtain a hiking map. Instead, we wandered down one of the marked trails and were able to get a better view of the summit and glaciers that surround the area. From a distance, most glaciers look like snow. As you get closer to them, they begin to look like ice. When you get as close as we were at the summit, you realize how very blue they are, similar to the blue of a

We ate dinner at the Mountaineer Café as the sun set on the glaciers, turning them an amazing shade blue. We enjoyed a delicious glass of local Reisling with our dinner and had the most unique cheesebu eaten. It was on a square ficocia bun, with a square burger patty, chipolte smoked bacon, about a ha lettuce, and the cheese toasted directly on the bun. It was delicious! We both remarked that it was th our dining lives we'd ever had a fine glass of wine with a cheeseburger.

Magnificent Mt. Cook

page 14

Hydrangeas in Haast

Drury Homestead

Drury Homestead

Bottlebrush at Drury

New Zealand blooms

page 52

random musings

and parting thoughts

page 53

Maine Perfection

Diana Lyn McGraw of Virginia Beach, Virginia

Diana and her two little explorers delighted in quality family time while hiking through a green woodland in Maine. Wanting to share the story of how her boys connected with the natural surroundings, Diana added handwritten journaling on inked tags tucked into pockets. She says, "We came back with so many photos and memorabilia. These fun pockets are perfect for displaying these important items."

To create a rustic type treatment, try square chipboard letters stitched with inked embroidery thread and adhered to your album's cover with strong adhesive. This adds visual interest as well as dimension. When planning your design, choose a color scheme that reflects your theme as Diana did here by using earthy brown and forest green. To further play upon the nature theme, add a fresh mix of paper and silk flowers. Resin-coated stickers can add a glossy touch.

My darling Boys,
I hope that you have enjoyed the trip to Maine as much as I did. I think that it is good for us to stop every once and a while and remind ourselves about the beauty around.
Nature is a beautiful thing... it is peaceful, serene, and it's perfect just the way it is. Your Daddy and I love you very much and these moments will last a life time.
♡ Mommy
MAINE
pERfEctIoN

Our Honeymoon (Mis)Adventure

Courtney Walsh of Winnebago, Illinois

Courtney and her husband were disappointed to find their honeymoon "love nest" a hopelessly dilapidated old cabin. Wanting to be sure everyone back home knew it was no exaggeration, she snapped photos of the ramshackle bungalow for full horrific effect. Finally able to look back and laugh (well, a little), Courtney was ready to scrapbook the experience. Not every vacation will be perfect, but document it anyway. You may come to find years later you will cherish the moments spent with loved ones even if events went awry. And, it will make for some interesting stories to share with future generations.

Our Love Nest

The Love Nest, they called it. We should've known by that alone we were in trouble. It took us hours to find the place with the directions they gave us. When we finally did, we wished we were still looking - this 'cabin in the woods' was more like a brown colored house that someone slapped some paint on and decorated with the furniture they were so happy to finally replace in their own house. We had no idea the cabins weren't cleaned by a professional service. It was just local people who rented the cabins out.
Never do this. Not a good idea.
First off, we were greeted by a pile of dog poo on the front porch. We thought that was a particularly nice touch. Then, we went inside and the smell was overwhelming. Basically, the place was one room with a half wall to section off the bathroom. But everything going on inside the bathroom was perfectly heard outside the bathroom because the wall didn't extend all the way to the ceiling.

The decorations in our cabin left much to be desired. They literally felt like cast-offs. Our own apartment back home was nicer. Of course, our apartment back home didn't have a hot tub on the deck out back, complete with a broken cover and half a tree sticking out the top. All I kept thinking was, "This is supposed to be our honeymoon." Which then led me to "I'm never using a travel agent again."
crazy

If you're using photos taken before the digital age, you may have to scan and re-size them in Photoshop if they're too large to fit as is. A two-ring album bound with ribbon is an easy format to work with and allows you to add plenty of creative touches. Use a coordinating paper line for continuity. Buttons and stickers adhered with pop dot adhesive can add dimension.

The decorations in our cabin left much to be desired. They literally felt like cast-offs. Our own apartment back home was nicer. Of course, our apartment back home didn't have a hot tub on the deck out back, complete with a broken cover and half a tree sticking out the top. All I kept thinking was, "This is supposed to be our honeymoon." Which then led me to "I'm never using a travel agent again."
crazy

Anatomy of Fly Fishing

Becky Fleck of Columbus, Montana

Fishing tackle, rods, waders and two loyal dog companions—Becky and her husband had everything they needed to make their fly fishing tour complete. Making their way to some of the best rivers in the West, Becky documented their fishing ventures in this 7" x 4.5" (18cm x 11cm) chipboard album.

Not all journaling has to be paragraph-style. In this example, Becky documented important details in bulleted-list format—but with a twist. She arranged her text to wrap around the circles that encompass an acrylic dome, which she filled with an arrangement of dry flies to emphasize her fishing theme. Mix playful patterned papers and don't be afraid to add feminine elements such as polka-dot ribbon or floral patterns.

MY GEAR LIST
STILLWATER RIVER ★ MT
paddy socks • nippers • zingers • lucky hat • zinc • net • gink • wading boots • fishing vest • tipet
MY WEAPON OF CHOICE
SNAKE RIVER ★ WY
St Croix 9ft 5wt 4-part rod • 9ft 3x leader • 4x tipet • lime green fly line • custom painted Orvis reel

MY BUG ARSENOL
SUNLIGHT RIVER ★ WY
adams • san juan worm • copper john • blue winged olive • royal wulff • red humpy • prince nymph
MY PARTNER IN CRIME
CLARKS FORK RIVER ★ WY
king of the short cast • best fishing buddy • chief bug selector • snag un-doer • local fishing guide

2007 Desk Calendar

Suzy Plantamura of Laguna Niguel, California

Suzy captures the majesty of Big Sur and the floral beauty of Butchart Gardens in this album-turned-desk calendar. Wanting to display her photos bright and big, but in a functional way, she took a three-ring binder and added chipboard pages for each month of the year. Her cover sports a tropical theme with velvet paper wrapping around the spine.

An easy way to format each calendar month is to use software such as Excel or Photoshop. If you want the main focus to be on your photos, keep embellishments to a minimum. Look to calendars or decorative datebooks you may already own for inspiration. Acrylic paint softly brushed on the edges of pages can add visual interest. A white gel pen works great for adding handwritten information to photos.

Butchart Gardens
Victoria Island
FEBRUARY
SUNDAY MONDAY TUESDAY WEDNESDAY THURSDAY FRIDAY SATURDAY
1 2 3
4 5 6 7 8 9 10
11 12 13 14 15 16 17
18 19 20 21 22 23 24
Valentine's Day
President's Day
25 26 27 28
MARCH
SUNDAY MONDAY TUESDAY WEDNESDAY THURSDAY FRIDAY
1 2
4 5 6 7 8 9
11 12 13 14 15 16
18 19 20 21 22
25 26 27 28 29
Big Sur, California

A View from the Old Course

Barb Hogan of Cincinnati, Ohio

A trip centered on a sporting event—whether it be your child's softball game up state or the Olympics in a far-off country—makes for a great travel album. Barb's once-in-a-lifetime experience at St. Andrew's Links deserved a place to document the fun, excitement and lush green Scottish soil of this golfer's paradise. Handmade cardstock pages and a chipboard cover are bound with four mini jump rings to compose a striking album.

Use a quote or famous saying on the cover or opening spread to set the tone. A fun way to include extra photos that don't fit into your basic design is to burn them onto a CD-ROM. Ribbons, rickrack, mini tags and a garden of patterned papers will add decorative touches. To add a flavor of authenticity, include a map, logo or clippings from a brochure or guidebook.

in THE HOLE
happy to be on the green and not in the North Sea!
The North Sea, Strong winds, Bunkers as deep as you are tall, Gorse that could shred Your hand, Time Limits, Hundreds of years of golfing history
COURSE MAP
EDEN ESTUARY
NEW COURSE
WEST SANDS
NORTH SEA
ST. ANDREWS LINKS
THE JUBILEE COURSE
SCORECARD
the bunkers were nearly as deep as my shoulders!
deep trap with the clubhouse in the back
St. Andrews, Scotland 1996
trip photo CD
Golf is so popular simply because it is the best game in the world at which to be bad. ~A.A. Milne
TEEING OFF
the Starter's Cottage
feeling a tad nervous...
It was quite surreal when waiting to tee off at the Starter's Cottage. To think that you are getting ready to play on the same turf as so many players throughout history, like Jack and Arnold and Tiger, was a bit overwhelming.

Whistler Vacation

Suzy Plantamura of Laguna Niguel, California

From downhill thrills to off-slope fun, vacation in Whistler, British Columbia, is an experience to savor. Using papers and accents in frosty, frozen blue and polar ice pink, Suzy was able to capture the chill and charm in an album dedicated to her family's annual trek to this winter wonderland.

If you've visited any place where the snow sparkles against brilliant blue skies, a chipboard album is the place to chronicle it. Snowflakes, glitter and polka-dot paper coordinate to emphasize the powder theme. For an interesting touch, try adding a sticker or rub-on, such as a snowflake gracefully floating on a child's tongue, over a photo to make it appear as if the element is a part of the photo. Journaling and quotes can be added to tags or envelopes peppered throughout. Don't forget fanciful ribbon and colorful rickrack to add that finishing touch.

For a unique cover treatment, try covering the chipboard with a piece of thin fiber-based specialty paper. Seal the edges with a light coat of dimensional glaze to prevent frayed edges. An oversized chipboard shape may be all it takes to add the perfect dash of visual interest. In this example, Suzy took a pre-made chipboard snowflake and sprinkled a generous helping of glitter to make it shimmer and shine.

Whistler Winter

Suzy Plantamura of Laguna Niguel, California

Camera TIPS

You may have only chance to get that perfect shot. Know how to manipulate the features of your camera, and arm yourself with basic photography principles before hitting the road.

- **Utilize the rule of thirds**
- **Use people and objects to establish proportion and scale**
- **Fill the frame with your subject**
- **Zoom in to capture detail**
- **Be aware of lighting**
- **Experiment with vertical, horizontal and extreme angles**
- **Capture people or places that reflect your unique photo-graphic vision**

Chapter five

Ticket TO FUN

Bumper cars and roller coasters, funnel cake and ice cream dots, postcards and souvenirs—the child in all of us delights in enjoyable excursions and curious adventures. When you find yourself on these quests for fun, remember to grab the camera and document each and every moment of wonder. A trip to a local zoo may turn into the perfect opportunity for creating an A-Z animal album that will serve as both a learning tool and a memory keepsake. Or perhaps a jaunt to a children's museum will provide inspiration for interactive elements within your pages. Turn the pages of this chapter to find great examples of albums that step outside the box and show how discovery, learning and fun make for wonderful family memories. So whether you're touching the delicate wings of a butterfly, collecting autographs from favorite Disney characters or strapping on your flippers and pretending your riding a wave with Shamu, document these adventures in albums you'll cherish for a lifetime.

our
VISIT
CHICAGO
CHILDREN'S
MUSEUM

Disneyland Autograph Book

May Flaum of Vacaville, California

May thought it would be a fun activity to bring an autograph book to Disneyland so her daughter could collect signatures from her favorite characters. She says, "I wanted a book that could be used to collect autographs and then once home, take apart, add photos and a few embellishments, and put back together as a completed album." Since it had to be tough enough to withstand the vacation, May constructed it from thick, sturdy pressed wood board.

The cover was tricky to cover because it had some slick finish on it initially. But May found some fun stationery paper (almost tissue thin), and decided to put a photo of her daughter surrounded by buttons on the cover to reinforce the idea that this is her autograph book. To seal everything in and add security to the buttons, May used a generous helping of perfect paper adhesive.

Down on the Farm

Michelle Van Etten of Pensacola, Florida

A happy little boy playing in the mud and skipping stones on the open farmland with his Nana is chronicled in this 6" x 6.5" (15cm x 16.5cm) spiral-bound album. To show the joy and laughter, Michelle used a bouncy mix of patterned papers dressed in stripes and polka dots.

EXPLORE
OAK LEAF
James you and Nana had so much fun on your nature walk. Down the hill at the farm is a small creek. You and Nana went down there to skip stones. You had so much fun playing in the mud and collecting stones. It was so sweet how you let Nana help you up. You have such a natural bond

Hidden tags work great for detailed journaling and fit conveniently into vertical or horizontal pockets. Paper flowers, resin-coated stickers and metal-rimmed words are quick and easy embellishments to add to album pages. For a cool type treatment, add three different colors of ink to large chipboard letters. Follow with an application of dimensional glaze for a glossy shine, as Michelle did for the word "farm" on her cover. For a different type of texture, tie small fabric strips instead of ribbon to the spiral binding.

Spring Break

Alecia Grimm of Atlanta, Georgia

Alecia's kids are transported back to 18th-century Colonial days as they browse and play in the Old Salem Children's Museum. With so many different scenes and backgrounds from the museum's many exhibits, Alecia needed to find a way to cohesively merge her photos. This post-bound album proved to be the perfect solution.

If you have pages that feature different colors or photos, keep the album unified by repeating techniques such as inking or distressing. Mix up chipboard letters by using different sizes, styles and colors. Word stickers and strip journaling are great ways to tell your story. In this example, Alecia used numbered journaling to list the amazing things the family saw at the museum.

Carnival

Vicki Boutin of Burlington, Ontario, Canada

Don't discount day trips or weekend getaways when creating travel albums. Vicki's family didn't travel far from home when they decided to spend the day at the carnival, but she knew the event was worthy of celebration. Festivals, trips to local parks, zoos or museums and even the circus are other great events to document.

Have fun experimenting with photos cropped into full circles or half circles. Circular shapes and repeating geometric patterns can add movement and energy. Add a rainbow of ribbons in carnival colors to embellish an otherwise standard jump ring. Place mini letter stickers around a circular element to move the eye across the page. Add the perfect finishing touch with a retro admission ticket to reinforce your theme.

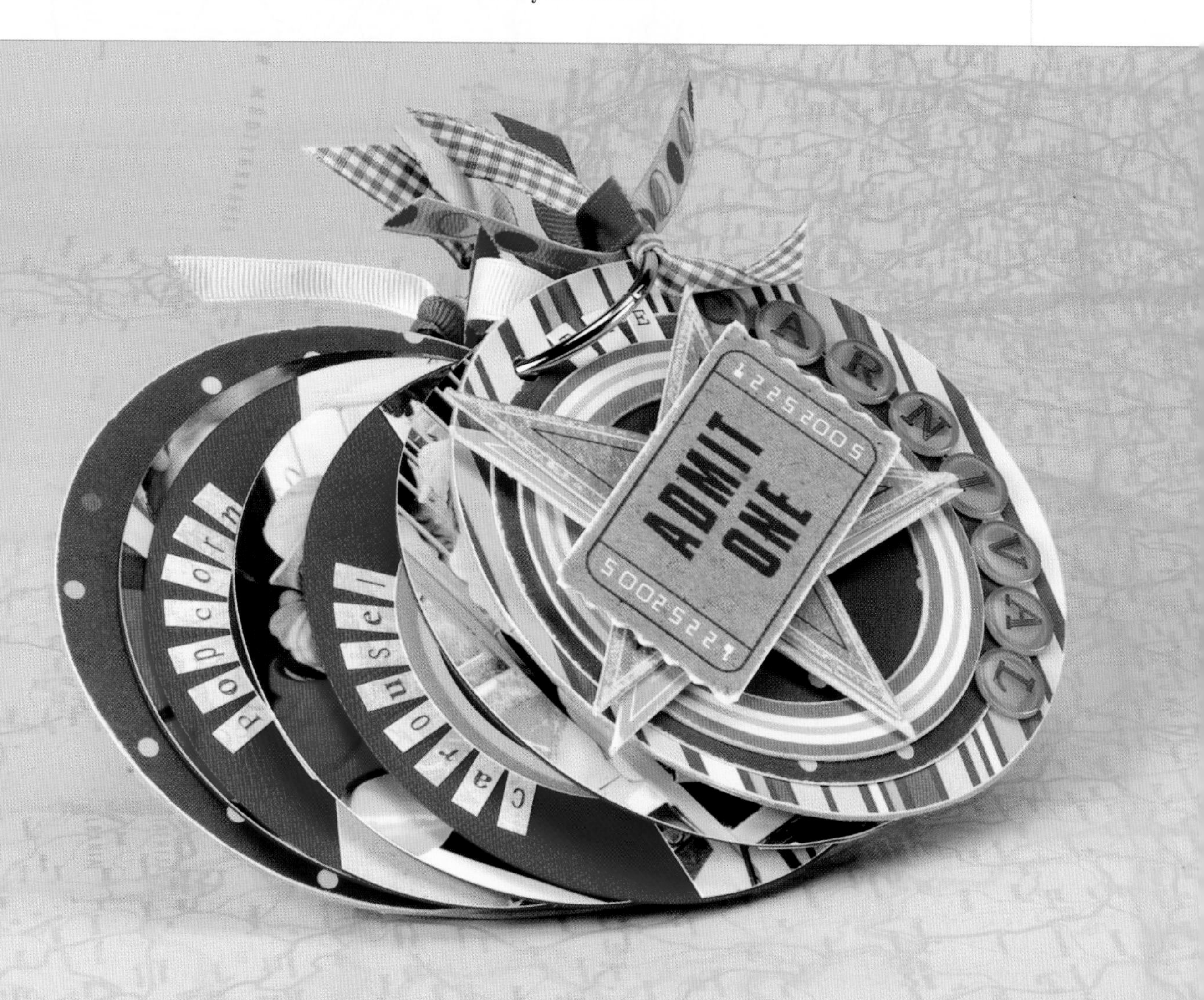

27 JUL 1999
ENTRY PERMIT EXEMPT
(4034)
10 MAY 1999
23 JUL 1999
As soon as we walked
through the gates, you were
ready to go!! When you got
on your 1st ride of the day
you laughed for
the entire ride!!
What a hoot!! The
two of you had a blast in the
Bumper Cars. I was an absolute
watching you guys
laugh and have
Fun!!
Round and Round
GAP
Bumper Cars

Mote Aquarium with Grandpa

Linda Harrison of Sarasota, Florida

A day of fun at a local aquarium is joyfully captured in this circular album. Wanting to be sure her son would enjoy looking through the album as much as she enjoyed making it, Linda set out to create something that would appeal to a child's curiosity. She also wanted to reinforce the special connection between generations as a way to document their family's heritage.

One of the exhibits you liked the most
was the Ray Touch Pool. Papa picked you
up an propped you on his knee so you could
better reach the rays and crabs that were
found in the tank. You both got really got
a kick out of touching all the sea life

A fun variation from traditional "documentation" is to use your album as way to tell a story. Because Linda wanted her son to be able to enjoy the album as soon as he was able to read, she kept the journaling simple and wrote it as narrative to spark his interest. Another fun element is the circular shape. You can easily crop photos with a craft knife to fit on album pages. Small patchworks of patterned paper and cardstock trimmed to reflect your theme (in this case water) will create an eye-pleasing design.

Butterfly Conservatory

Vicki Boutin of Burlington, Ontario, Canada

Vicki likes to "collect bits of life" in her scrapbooks. She created this album by fusing together a variety of different shapes and sizes of tags constructed of chipboard and cardstock. She created the butterfly using a hand-held cutter and template. She then layered the shapes and monogram with foam adhesive. Jewels and a twisted cardstock strip complete the custom butterfly. An endearing photo showcases a gorgeous specimen perched on child's shoulder.

Create a custom-made shape to clearly communicate your theme, and use dimensional adhesive to make it pop off the page. Tag albums are easier to approach if you have multiple photos and little-to-no memorabilia. They provide room for a variety of photos and journaling, which can be added as desired. Journaling can wrap around or be on the back of a tag.

Ft. Wayne Zoo

Greta Hammond of Goshen, Indiana

A day of riding horses, feeding goats and getting to know the entire animal kingdom at the Fort Wayne Zoo brought smiles to the faces of Greta's young children. Wanting to create both a keepsake and a fun interactive educational tool, Greta embellished photos from the excursion in this 7.5" x 5.25" (19cm x 13cm) spiral-bound album.

Organizing your album in an A-Z format makes it easy and fun to come up with page themes. Of course, there may be a few letters of the alphabet where you'll have to get really creative but, hey, that's what this hobby is all about, right? Creating an album in this style can also serve as a learning device for younger children who are learning their ABCs. Adhere chipboard letters in the center of circles to make them pop off the page. A mix of zig-zag, striped and polka-dot papers will add movement and rhythm to each page.

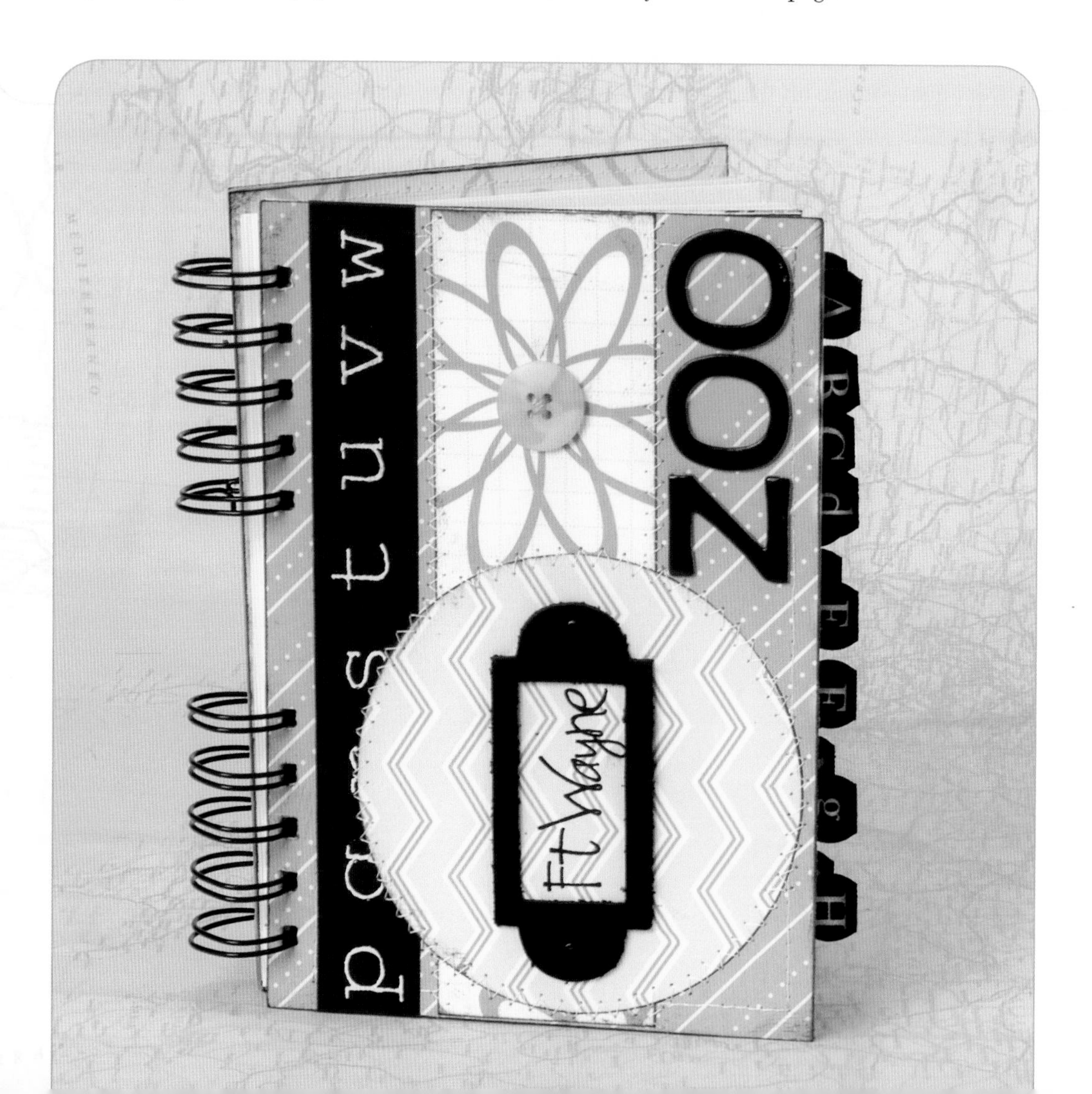

G
f
e
D
c
b
a
g
is for
GOATS
h
is for
HORSE
RIDES
H
N
K
I

Chicago Children's Museum

Courtney Walsh of Winnebago, Illinois

The Chicago Children's Museum has many interactive elements for kids to play and learn with. So Courtney cleverly decided to carry that idea over into her album. Since this album is for her children, she wanted to create fun things using photos from the trip.

A great idea is to model a page after a game or game board. Finding inspiration from a giant tic tac toe board at the museum, Courtney created the game board on the right page using Velcro to make the photos removable. Use multi-colored patterned papers with repeated geometric shapes to add rhythm and unity, and dimensional adhesive to make elements pop off the page. Add a photo of a sign or logo to your album's cover to add instant information about the place or setting.

Sea World

Suzy Plantamura of Laguna Niguel, California

The magnificent mammals of Sea World make a splash on the pages of this circular chipboard album. Using a blue and black color scheme to match her Shamu photos, Suzy shows the wonder and excitement of this world-renown excursion.

If you want to save time trimming at the craft table, arrange your photos in image-editing software, print onto photo paper and then crop and adhere to the page background. This will give you more freedom in your designs and will also allow you to zoom in on particular elements or features you find visually appealing. Another fun idea is to include a smaller inset photo over a large one. On the center page on the right, Suzy shows how to effectively illustrate scale and proportion in a photograph by shooting the trainer next to Shamu, the killer whale. There are all sorts of fun photography tricks you can experiment with. Allow the photos to be the star of your pages by including only minimal embellishments.

SEAWORLD
SeaWorld has quickly become our favorite theme park for many reasons.
We love the animals, the shows, the rides! getting wet in the Soak Zones!
LOVERS
SHAMU
SHAMU
I love the Shamu show. There is so much energy as the crowd shouts "Shamu Shamu" and he splashes with his tail!

Chapter six

Globetrotter's Paradise

Are you someone who's filled with insatiable wanderlust? Have you been lucky enough to have had the opportunity to summit to the top of the Eiffel Tower, tour the galleries of the Louvre, pay your regards to Buckingham Palace, or stand in awe at the Taj Mahal? Perhaps these or other destinations are on that ever-growing list of places you'd like see. On the pages that follow, you'll discover a variety of new album ideas from destinations around the world. Learn fun ways to punch up your journaling, techniques for including tags and memorabilia in album pages and fresh ideas for decorating album covers. You'll also see ways to break out of the traditional album format with a decorated vintage suitcase and a mini album resembling train tickets. So whether you're on an expedition to see the wonders of the world or just taking a day trip up to that historic town off the beaten path, document your travels in albums that will tell your unique travel stories.

pull
pull
pull
pull
pull
It's a great big
World
out there.
a bird's eye view

Places Scrapbooking Has Taken Me

May Flaum of Vacaville, California

If you've ever traveled for a passion or hobby, put the photos to good use in an album that shares your adventure. May finds excitement in traveling to teach and spend time with her crop-happy friends. She celebrates their adventures in an 8" x 8" (20cm x 20cm) album constructed of cardstock and patterned paper.

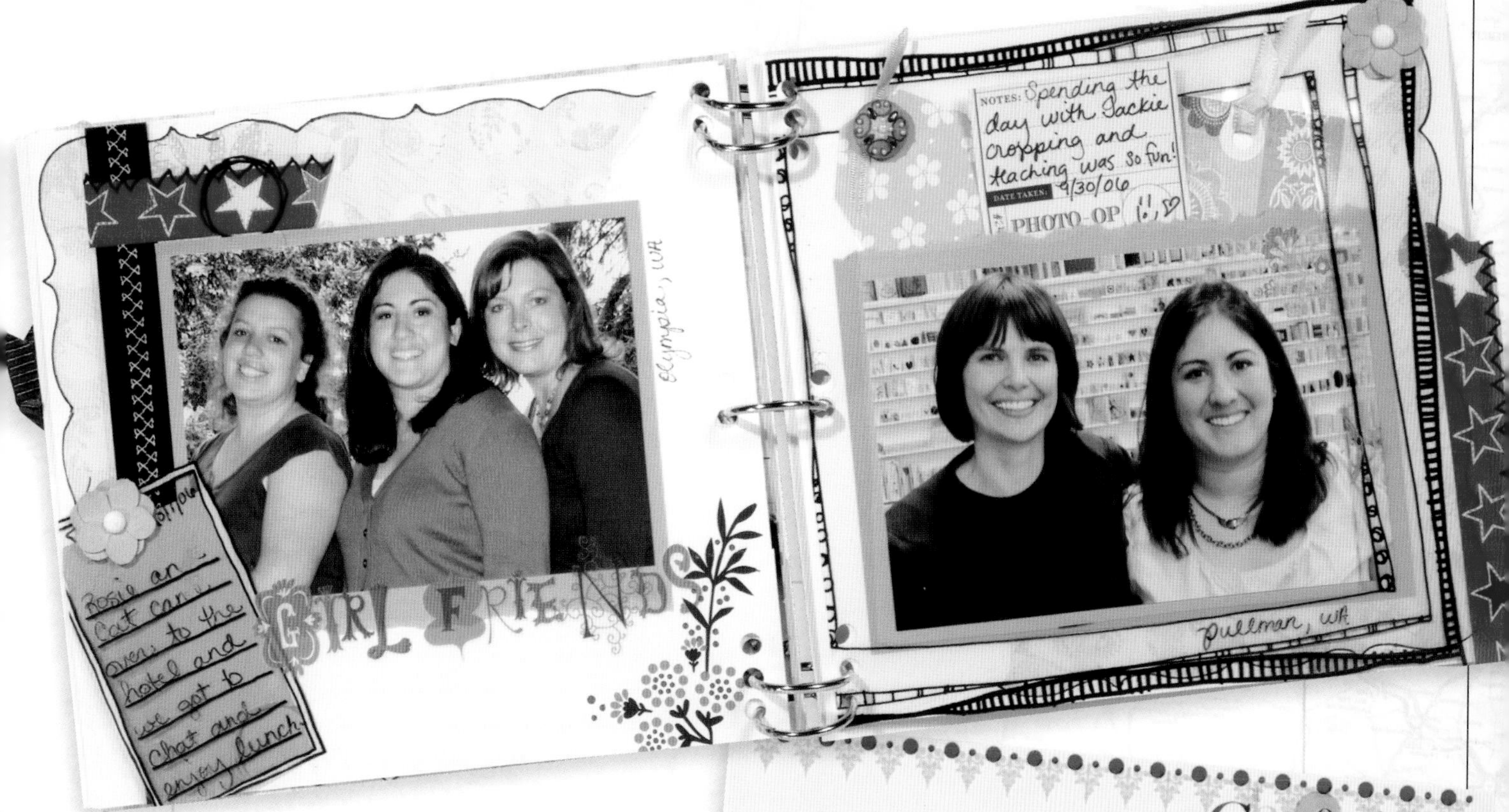

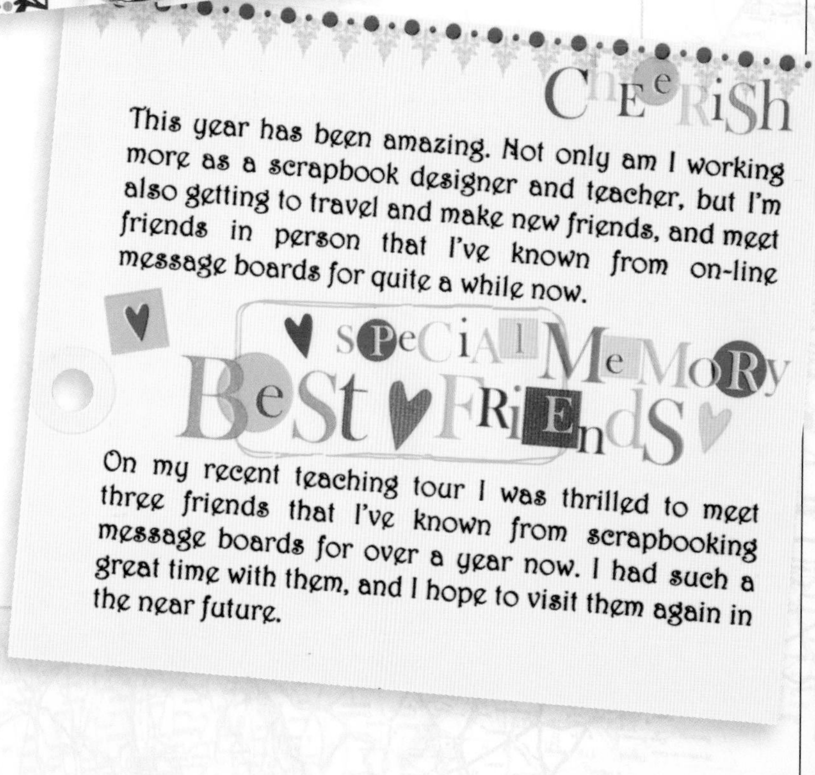

A fun idea is to add a map to document your travels. An easy way to do this is to save a map from Yahoo maps, then using Photoshop Elements add stars or other symbols to show where you've been and where you're going. Don't forget to include yourself in photos to share the joy you experienced while traveling to pursue your passion.

Cherish

This year has been amazing. Not only am I working more as a scrapbook designer and teacher, but I'm also getting to travel and make new friends, and meet friends in person that I've known from on-line message boards for quite a while now.

Special Memory

Best Friends

On my recent teaching tour I was thrilled to meet three friends that I've known from scrapbooking message boards for over a year now. I had such a great time with them, and I hope to visit them again in the near future.

The Story of Rhyolite

Caroline Ikeji of Alhambra, California

From the Gold Rush of settlers in the early 1900s to the adrenaline rush of sightseers who visit today, the history of this boomtown-turned-ghost town is chronicled in Caroline's chipboard album. She initially thought distressing techniques and dull colors would work for a ghost town theme, but decided to be adventurous with brighter colors and retro papers that stay true to her personal style.

Choose accents that complement the colors of your photos and paper, and also add a bit of texture. If you're going for a vintage feel, use labels for title blocks. Felt flowers, polka-dot ribbon and journaling printed on strips can add further enrichment. If your album shares pieces of the past, use each spread to focus on a different historical element. Viewers will be intrigued by the wealth of information and photos that support it.

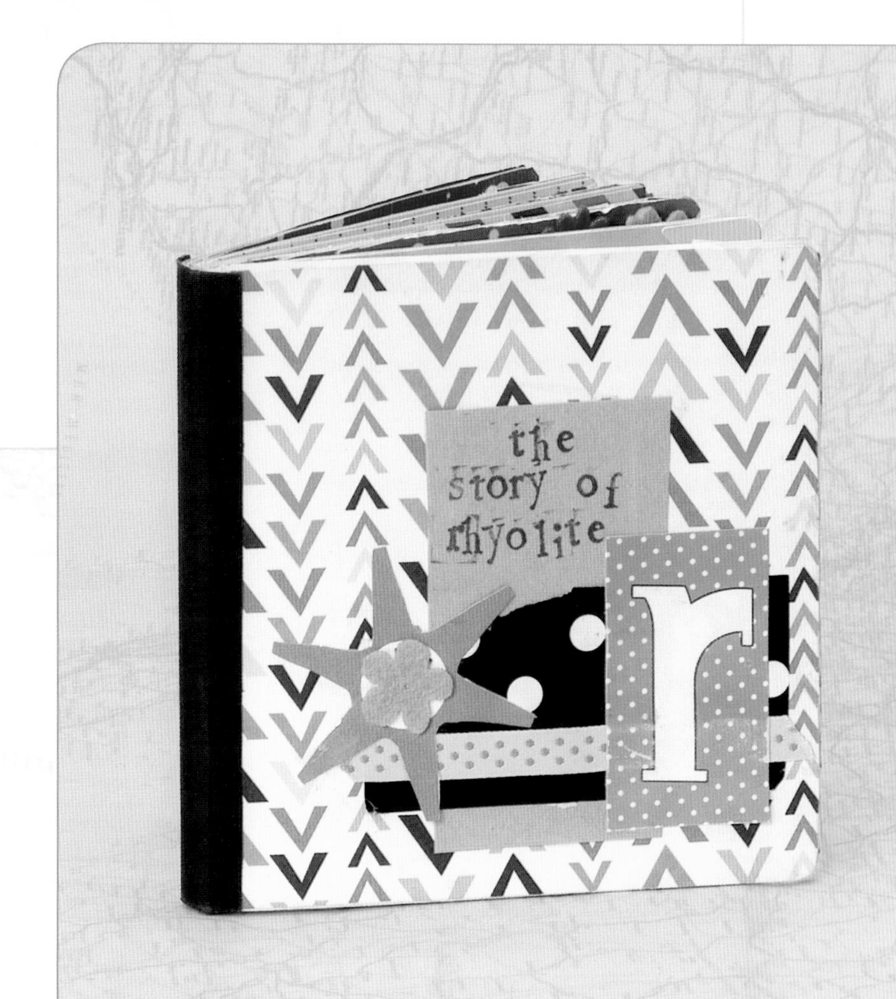

Rhyolite was serviced by
two railroads - the Las
Vegas and Tonopah,
and Tonopah and Tidewater
railroads. To accommodat
them, two train depots
were built. After the railroads no longer serviced
Rhyolite, one depot was
used as space for a
casino and restaurant,
then later a residence.
The depot still stands.
Rhyolite
train depot

The bottle house greets visitors as they first arrive in
Rhyolite. The house was built with 50,000 beer,
wine, and whiskey bottles. Built in 1906 by resident
Tom Kelley, it is only one of three such structures
remaining. It is currently undergoing restoration.
bottle house
Rhyolite, NV

Lazy 5 Ranch

Michelle Van Etten of Pensacola, Florida

Michelle wanted to give her son a book he could look at years to come to remember their family trip to the Lazy 5 Ranch. With so many of the animals being classified as endangered species, the opportunity gave her even more reason to photograph and document the experience. To add interesting details to the album in a creative way, she printed the animals' facts on pull-out tags below the photos.

A double spiral-bound album offers a wealth of design possibilities. Because one side flips vertical and other horizontal, you can mix it up by featuring large photographs of people or animals on one side, and interesting facts and journaling details on the other. Use coordinating papers, ribbons and paper flowers to keep a cohesive feel.

Mediterranean Summer Cruising 2000

Vicki Boutin of Burlington, Ontario, Canada

Open Vicki's album and retreat to the translucent waters, jasmine-scented breezes and tidy cobbled streets of the Mediterranean. Wanting to capture the true essence of her vivid adventure, Vicki showcases the many textures and facets of the richly hued stretch of this famed coastline.

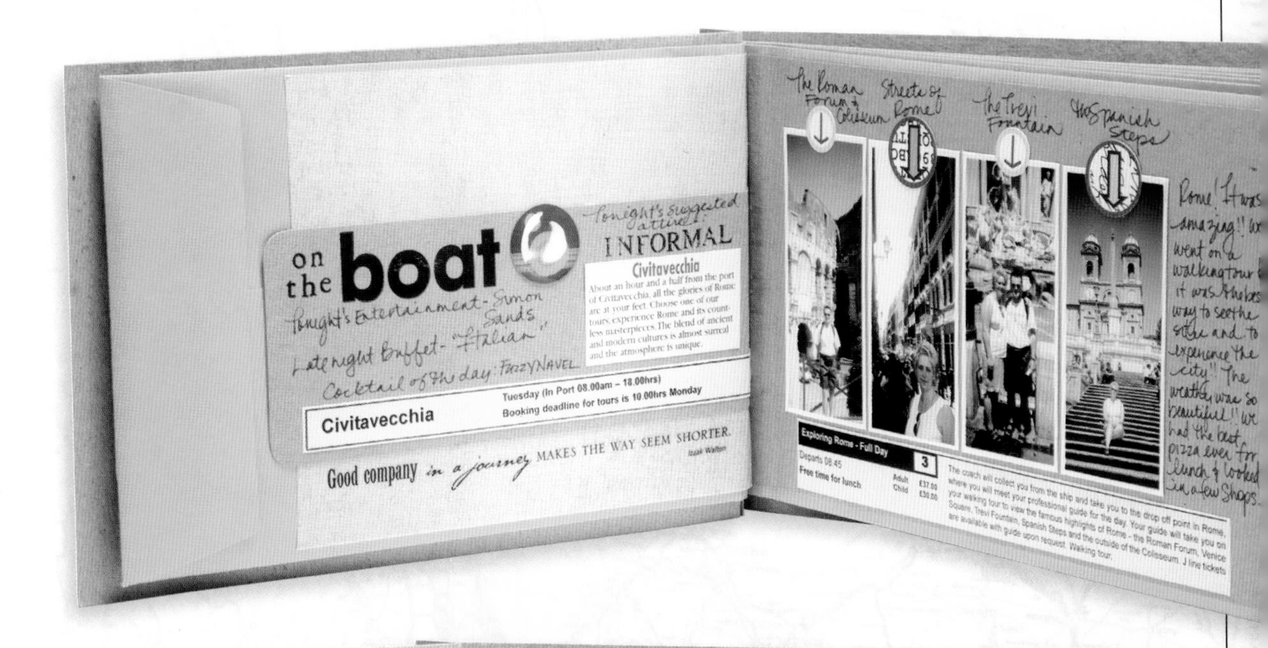

Stunning photography can tell a story on its own, but don't be afraid to employ a few creative techniques to add to your illustration. One fun and functional idea is to construct the interior pages of your album from manila envelopes. The envelopes serve as pockets to handily store journaling and memorabilia leaving ample space for photographs and other design elements on the fronts and backs. Another clever idea is to feature your itinerary for an at-a-glance peek at your trip's adventures. Handwritten journaling, a map and evocative photos add further interest. Mix and match Vicki's travel ideas with your own to create a one-of-a-kind album that shows a spectacular view.

Trains

Caroline Ikeji of Alhambra, California

This 4" x 4" (10cm x 10cm) loose-leaf album bound by a single jump ring mimics the look and feel of the train tickets sold to passengers riding the Japanese rail system. Caroline used a mixture of bright, eye-pleasing colors to convey a childhood feeling as the trains remind her so much of her own childhood visits to Japan.

Instead of cropping patterned paper or cardstock, create your own "papers" by using image-editing software to design your pages and then print them onto the same paper as your photos. Use minimal embellishments such as buttons or ribbon tied through a punched hole to dress up the page with texture. For a uniform journaling technique, record facts or figures (such as the type of train and destination in Caroline's example) as well as your own personal impressions or recollections of the experience. Include photos spanning several years to illustrate the passage of time.

nanki
type: express
destination: Nagoya to Mie and Wakayama
photo taken: 1993
Nanki made up the last leg of trips between Tokyo and grandma's. It is also the train to get to my dad's hometown in Wakayama. The Nanki is a wide view train. If you're lucky enough to sit in the green car, you get a very nice view.
type: local
destination: in and around Tokyo, Chiba
photo taken: 1988
We took the Joban-sen on to my aunt Shii-chan's house from Tokyo. We took it to get from Tokyo to Kashiwa (in Chiba) when grandma lived there too.
joban sen

Bird's Eye View

Becky Fleck of Columbus, Montana

Becky's accordion-style album is constructed of patterned paper, ribbon and transparency. But no one will argue that the photos are the true gem of her creation. Becky and her husband had the opportunity to take a helicopter tour where she captured the amazing flora and fauna of this New Zealand mountain range. Magnetic straps tied to ribbon hold the accordion album closed. She tucked journaling into tags to tell the story of each set of photos.

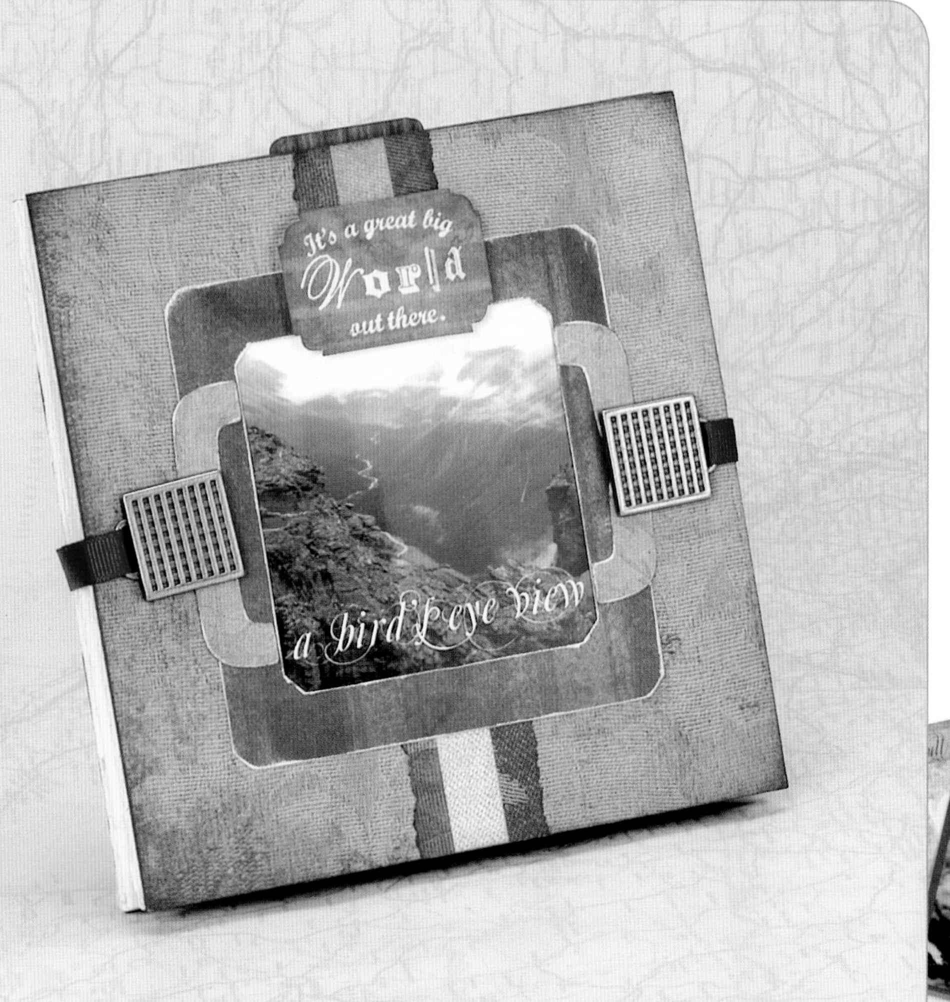

There's just something inspiring about shooting from above. This will require more planning as you'll have to be lucky enough to take a helicopter tour as Becky did, or find your way to the nearest mountaintop. But the task is not impossible. Becky offers a tip on capturing the perfect photo once air bound, "I also used two different lenses—a wide angle and a 75/300 for the close-up shots." Know how to manipulate the features of your camera to get the best shots. And if you're looking for a fun way to display them, try adhering them to tags tucked into pockets. This allows viewers to easily pull them out for an up-close view.

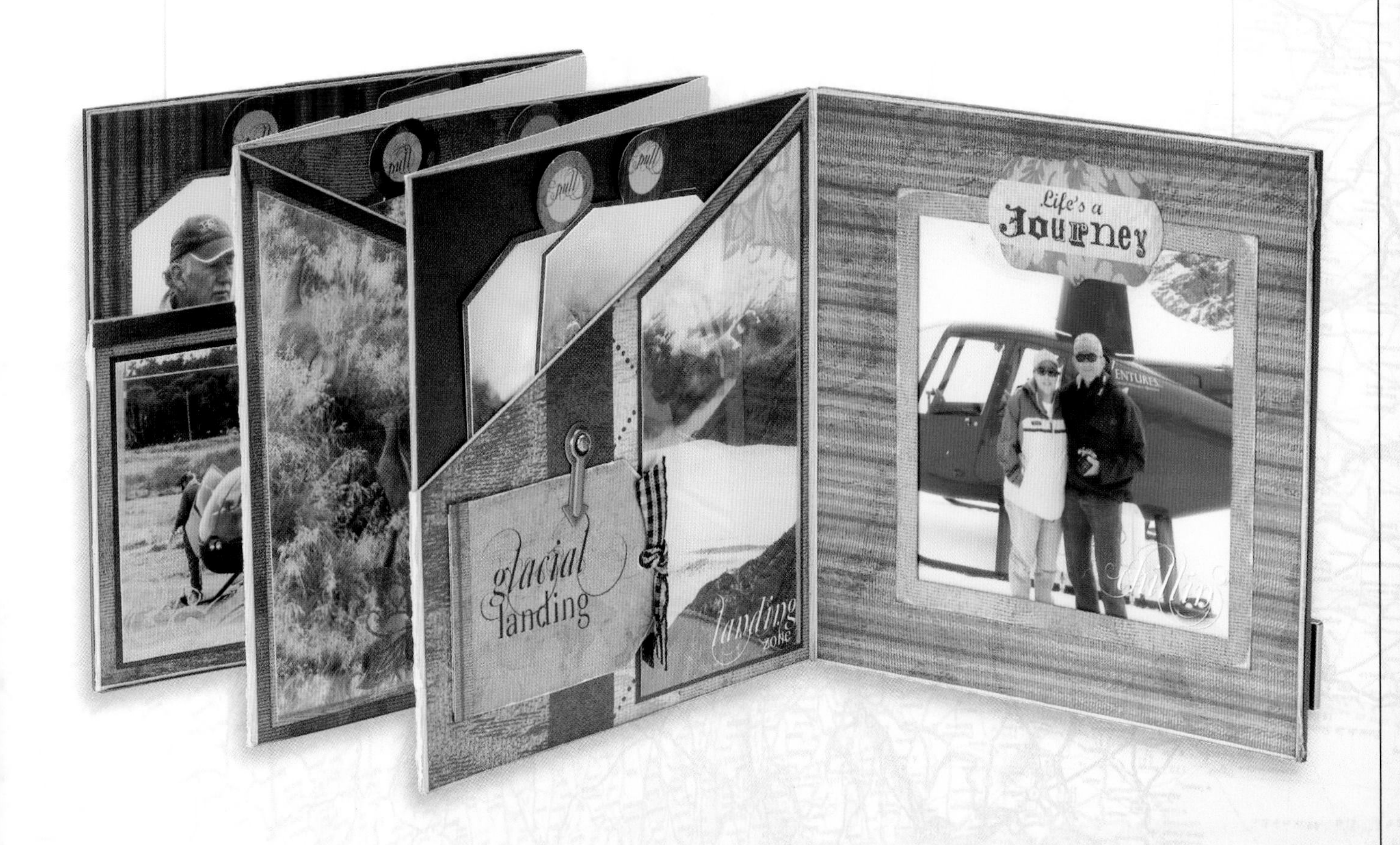

Mexico

Alecia Grimm of Atlanta, Georgia

Alecia infuses her vacation memories with the spirit of Mexican design in this 10" x 9" (25cm x 23cm) post-bound album. Photos of Aztec pyramids warmed by a desert sun fill the interior pages creating a striking composition.

An easy way to decorate an album cover is to use stickers or images representing your theme. Alecia says, "I found images that paint a vivid picture of Mexico. I used decoupage medium to adhere and seal everything. Beads, shells and coins were used to add texture and authenticity." Select colors and patterns that match your theme. In this example, Alecia chose an album in radiant red and selected patterned papers that resemble Mexican tiles for the interior spread. Add handwritten journaling for a personal touch.

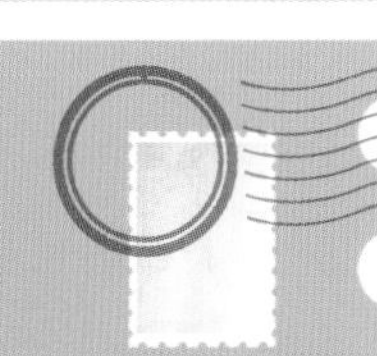

The Well-Read Traveler

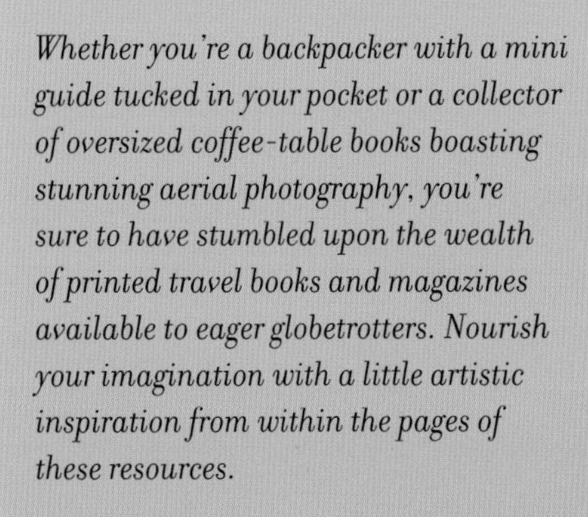

Whether you're a backpacker with a mini guide tucked in your pocket or a collector of oversized coffee-table books boasting stunning aerial photography, you're sure to have stumbled upon the wealth of printed travel books and magazines available to eager globetrotters. Nourish your imagination with a little artistic inspiration from within the pages of these resources.

- Memory Makers Travel Scrapbooks **(Volume 10, Number 2)**
- Creating Vacation Scrapbook Pages **(Memory Makers Books)**
- The Photographer's Travel Guide **by William Manning (Writer's Digest Books)**
- How to Take Great Vacation Photographs **by John Hedgecoe (Collins & Brown)**
- **National and local travel magazines such as** National Geographic Traveler **or** Budget Travel

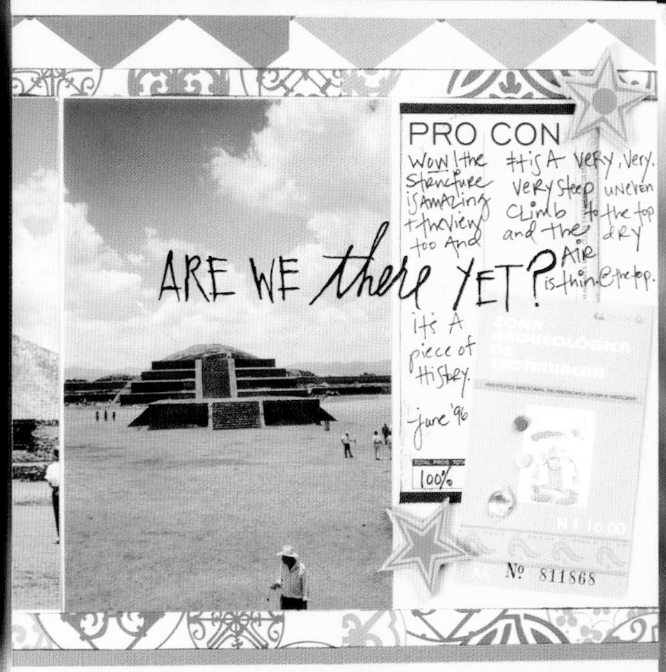

Paraguay

Alecia Grimm of Atlanta, Georgia

Do you come back from vacation with a multitude of photos and in search of good way to display them? Sometimes we have more photos than we have time to scrapbook. Alecia sought a solution to the photo-overload conundrum by simply organizing them according to destination or theme into pre-made post-bound albums. She got really creative when she decided to put the albums into a decorated suitcase boasting her own personal touch.

The suitcase in this example was purchased from a scrapbook manufacturer, but garage sales, flea markets, thrift stores, auctions, estate sales and eBay are also other places to locate a vintage-style case. Embellish with wrappers, bottle caps, tickets and stickers brought back from your journey. In addition to the albums, you can also store souvenirs or other memorabilia collected from your trip.

Architecture Through My Lens

Barb Hogan of Cincinnati, Ohio

There are times when a photographer knows something special is happening in front of the camera. For Barb, this "a-ha" moment occurs when she stumbles upon architectural splendor, whether it be a lofty castle tower or an enclave of houses tucked quietly away in an old-world village. For her, the architecture of the world is the treasure of treasures. By focusing on a single element of travel—such as architecture, people or landscapes—you can easily combine pictures from different places without sacrificing consistency.

stonehenge, Wiltshire England
circa 3100 BC
i love taking photos of archetecture,
whether it be ancient or modern,
building or bridge, stone or glass.
This is a collection of some of my
favorites... thru my own lens

An amazing album calls for an amazing cover. One effective, clever and fun technique is to combine digital tricks with traditional crafting. Barb's cover, designed on the computer and then printed, is a stunning example of how this can be achieved. To add a bit of texture, choose a design element (in this case the scrolls) to ink and then emboss with clear embossing powder. The remainder of the album is created in harmonious simplicity. Strips of patterned paper and handwritten journaling are the perfect complement to a montage of photos showing a painterly view.

European Architecture

Barb Hogan of Cincinnati, Ohio

Postcard CHRONICLES

Relive your travel adventures by capturing the moment with these journaling tips and techniques.

- Keep a chronological log of each day
- Jot down facts, history and trivia
- Tell a story: Recall the progression of events in an engaging narrative
- Use quotes, poems and sayings
- Record the basics: who, what, when, where, why and how
- Write home: Mail postcards to yourself from the road
- Employ the five senses to add dimension to the tale

Hit the OPEN ROAD

Page 10
Trips to Kansas *Greta Hammond*
Supplies: Patterned paper (Imagination Project); chipboard letters (Heidi Swapp); letter stickers (EK Success); letter stamps (PSX); buttons (Autumn Leaves); flowers (American Crafts); pen; cardstock; Times New Roman font (Microsoft)

Page 12
Starting Over *Brooke Bartimioli*
Supplies: Patterned paper (7 Gypsies, ANW Crestwood, BasicGrey, Chatterbox, Creating Keepsakes, Creative Imaginations, K&Co., Karen Foster, My Mind's Eye, Paper Love, Rusty Pickle); rub-on accents (7 Gypsies, BasicGrey, Karen Foster, Making Memories); stamps (Plaid, Provo Craft, Rubber Stampede); sticker accents (EK Success, Making Memories); brads; label maker (Dymo); clips, knob, rings, tags (7 Gypsies); acrylic and crackle paint; adhesive foam; dye and pigment ink; foil wine wrap, book binding (unknown); twine; pen; cardstock

Page 14
European Road Trips *Barb Hogan*
Supplies: Patterned paper (7 Gypsies, Anna Griffin, BasicGrey); coasterboard shapes (Imagination Project); brads; dye and pigment ink; dimensional paint; corner rounder; pens; cardstock; Old Typewriter font (Internet download)

Page 16
Road Trip by the Numbers *Linda Harrison*
Supplies: Album (Maya Road); patterned paper (KI Memories); die-cut letters (QuicKutz); letter stickers (Sticker Studio); pens; cardstock

Page 18
The Road Trip Home *Eileen Aber*
Supplies: Album (Canson); patterned paper (American Crafts, BasicGrey); maps (Rand McNally); rhinestone letters (Mark Richards); chipboard shapes (Imagination Project); rub-on accents (Chatterbox, Die Cuts With A View); round tags (EK Success); brads; word stickers (Making Memories); state stickers (Smile Makers); dye and pigment ink; cardstock; American Typewriter font (Microsoft)

Pages 20, 22
The Bus Diaries *Alecia Grimm*
Supplies: Patterned paper (Wubie Prints); mesh (Magic Mesh); letter stickers (American Crafts, Die Cuts With A View, Doodlebug, Making Memories); chipboard letters (Heidi Swapp); transparencies (Creative Imaginations, Hambly); quote tags (My Mind's Eye); metal charms (Nunn Designs); clips, travel stickers (Making Memories); metal tabs, photo turns, rub-ons, stickers (7 Gypsies); book ring, brads, button, pigment ink; ribbon (unknown); staples; pen; cardstock

Savvy IN THE CITY

Page 26
London Expedition *Diana Lyn McGraw*
Supplies: Patterned paper (KI Memories); letters (Bazzill, Paper Studio); floral accents (Prima, Teters); word transparency (Heidi Swapp); brads; label maker (Dymo); photo corners (Making Memories); rub-on accents (BasicGrey); album, ribbon (unknown); dye ink; corner rounder; pen; cardstock

Page 28
I Heart NY *Becky Fleck*
Supplies: Hand-cut wood base and frame (artist's own design); patterned paper (Cosmo Cricket); acrylic paint; dye ink; book rings; pen; cardstock; Garamond font (Microsoft); Pea Jenny Script font (Internet download)

Page 30
Cities of Europe *Linda Harrison*
Supplies: Patterned paper, ribbon (Chatterbox); chipboard letters (Making Memories); flowers (Prima); rhinestones (KI Memories); acrylic paint; pen; cardstock; Brainless font (Two Peas in a Bucket)

Page 32

Our Trip to Niagara Falls *Vicki Boutin*
Supplies: Chipboard book and accents (Fancy Pants); patterned paper (Scenic Route); acrylic letters (Heidi Swapp); bottle cap letters (Li'l Davis); letter stickers (EK Success, Karen Foster, Making Memories); rub-on letters (Daisy D's, Making Memories); clear dots (Cloud 9); book rings; sandpaper; pen; camera and coupons (Niagra Falls memorabilia)

Page 34

Washington, D.C. *Caroline Ikeji*
Supplies: Album (Junkitz); patterned paper (Chatterbox, Die Cuts With A View, MOD, Scenic Route); chipboard stars (Deluxe Designs, Heidi Swapp); buttons, number stickers, rub-on accents (American Crafts); letter and number stamps (Magnetic Poetry); dye ink; page tabs (unknown); cardstock; Bradley's Hand font (Microsoft)

Page 36

My Favorite Cities *May Flaum*
Supplies (Boston): Patterned paper (Scenic Route); map of Boston (unknown); letter stamps (Fontwerks); pigment ink; rickrack (May Arts); sticker accents (EK Success); brads; gold leafing pen; pen; cardstock; BoSox, CAC Shoshoni brush, French Script, Old English Text fonts (Internet download); Doodle Frame font (Autumn Leaves); Times New Roman font (Microsoft)

Supplies (Savannah): Patterned paper (7 Gypsies); letter stickers (Mustard Moon); flowers (Prima); rub-on accents (BasicGrey); brads; twill; decorative scissors; digital flourish brush (Designer Digitals); pen; cardstock; Garamond font (Microsoft)

Pages 38, 40

2 Travel *Suzy Plantamura*
Supplies: Album, rhinestone letter stickers (Creative Imaginations); patterned paper (Autumn Leaves, Fiskars, K&Co., My Mind's Eye, Three Bugs in a Rug); transparency (My Mind's Eye); epoxy letters (Me & My Big Ideas); rub-on letters (Li'l Davis, Making Memories, Me & My Big Ideas); plastic words (Heidi Swapp); word stickers (Making Memories); rub-on accents (Autumn Leaves, Die Cuts With A View, Fontwerks, K&Co., Me & My Big Ideas, My Mind's Eye); plastic tab (Artistic Expressions); ribbon (Making Memories, Maya Road); corner rounder, dye and pigment ink; staples, tags (unknown); marker, cardstock

Life's a Beach

Page 44

Cape Hatteras *Courtney Walsh*
Supplies: Patterned paper, flowers, letter stickers (Chatterbox); buttons (Wal-Mart); brads, ribbon (unknown); pigment ink; circle punch; corner rounder; pen; cardstock

Page 46

Moments 2 Remember *Diana Lyn McGraw*
Supplies: Patterned paper, ribbon (All My Memories); patterned transparency (My Mind's Eye); mailbox letters (Making Memories); rub-on letters (Heidi Swapp); door knob accent (7 Gypsies); floral accents (Prima); brads; dye ink; album (unknown); pen; cardstock

Page 48

Hawaii Postcard Album *Caroline Ikeji*
Supplies: Album (Paperchase); patterned paper (American Crafts, BasicGrey, KI Memories, My Mind's Eye, SEI); chipboard letters, journaling tags (Heidi Swapp); letter stickers (Die Cuts With A View, KI Memories); flowers (American Crafts, Doodlebug); brads, buttons (American Crafts); ribbon (American Crafts, Fancy Pants, KI Memories, SEI); rub-on accents (American Crafts, Imagination Project); sticker accents (KI Memories, Scrapworks); pen; cardstock

Page 50

Pensacola Beach *Michelle Van Etten*
Supplies: Album (Rusty Pickle); chipboard monogram, patterned paper (BasicGrey); letter stickers (BasicGrey, Making Memories); flowers (Prima); decorative brads (Karen Foster); journaling tag stamp (Autumn Leaves); resin stickers (All My Memories); ribbon (Shoebox Trims); rub-on accents (Heidi Swapp, My Mind's Eye); glossy topcoat (Ranger); adhesive foam; pen

Page 52

Our Faves and Memories *Linda Harrison*
Supplies: Album (C&T Publishing); patterned paper (American Crafts); die-cut letters and shapes (QuicKutz); binding tape (EK Success); ribbons (American Crafts, Doodlebug); pen; cardstock

Page 54

2 If By Sea *Becky Fleck*
Supplies: Paper Mache round box, patterned paper, rub-on and sticker accents, tags, vintage buttons (Melissa Frances); chipboard (BasicGrey, We R Memory Keepers); buttons (Doodlebug, Making Memories); beads (Darice, Mill Hill); glass beads, shells (souvenirs from New Zealand); acrylic paint; crackle finish; chalk; glossy top coat (Ranger); circle cutter; cardstock; Colwell, Honey Script fonts (Internet download)

Pages 56, 58

Michigan Travel Box *Hanni Baumgardner*
Supplies: Cardboard box (Expo Intl.); letter stickers (Making Memories); letter stamps (Magnetic Poetry, Making Memories); mesh (Magic Mesh); ribbon (Offray); flowers (Prima); buttons, felt, shells (unknown); acrylic paint; adhesive foam; decoupage medium; pen; cardstock

A Natural attraction

Page 62

Have Fly Rod, Will Travel *Becky Fleck*
Supplies: Patterned paper (Chatterbox, Southworth); glass beads (souvenir from New Zealand); waxed binding cord; japanese screw punch; cardstock; Goudy Old Style font (Microsoft); Zapfino title font (Internet download)

Page 64

Maine Perfection *Diana Lynn McGraw*
Supplies: Album (Rusty Pickle); patterned paper, resin stickers, ribbons (Stemma); chipboard letters (Heidi Swapp, Rusty Pickle); floral accents (Heidi Swapp, Prima); binder clip; brads; tags; pen; cardstock

Page 66

Our Honeymoon (Mis)adventure *Courtney Walsh*
Supplies: Album (Junkitz); letter stickers, patterned paper, sticker accents (Chatterbox); buttons (Autumn Leaves); ribbon (unknown); corner punch; decorative scissors; dye ink; embroidery floss; cardstock

Page 68

Anatomy of Fly Fishing *Becky Fleck*
Supplies: Album (7 Gypsies); die-cut shapes, patterned paper (Crate Paper); clear title letters (Heidi Swapp); rub-on accents (American Crafts, BasicGrey); ribbon (Shoebox Trims); acrylic dome lid (Provo Craft); acrylic paint; book binding tape (Making Memories); circle cutter; dye ink; fly fishing hooks (artist's own design); sandpaper; cardstock; Apple Garamond, Stamp Act fonts (Internet download)

Page 70

2007 Desk Calendar *Suzy Plantamura*
Supplies: Patterned paper (ANW Crestwood, Autumn Leaves, Karen Foster, Me & My Big Ideas, My Mind's Eye, NRN Designs, Rouge de Garance); velvet paper (SEI); plastic letters (Heidi Swapp); acrylic paint; album, ribbon, rickrack (unknown); pen; cardstock

Page 72

A View from the Old Course *Barb Hogan*
Supplies: Album covers (Junkitz); patterned paper (Chatterbox); letter stickers, tags (BasicGrey); rub-on letters (Imagination Project); book rings; brads; dye ink; pen; vellum; cardstock

Pages 74, 76

Whistler Vacation 2004 *Suzy Plantamura*
Supplies: Album (Maya Road); large chipboard snowflakes, glitter letter stickers (Making Memories); patterned paper (FiberMark, KI Memories, Making Memories, Paper Salon); snowflake accents (Heidi Swapp, Me & My Big Ideas); rhinestone circle accent (Heidi Swapp); ribbon (KI Memories, Making Memories, Me & My Big Ideas); rickrack (Doodlebug); epoxy accents (KI Memories); brads; vellum envelope (unknown); paperclip; glitter; dye ink; pens

Ticket TO FUN

Page 80

Disneyland Autograph Album *May Flaum*

Supplies: Pressed wooden album (unknown); patterned paper (Cloud 9, Marcel Schurman); acrylic circle stickers (Cloud 9); letter stickers (Making Memories); buttons (Autumn Leaves); book rings; corner punch; glitter; pen; ribbons; cardstock

Page 82

Down on the Farm *Michelle Van Etten*

Supplies: Chipboard album and letters (Rusty Pickle); epoxy stickers, patterned paper, tabs (All My Memories); fabric (Wal-Mart); ribbon (All My Memories, Michaels); silk flowers (Prima); large nature quotes (My Mind's Eye); resin stickers (Stemma); adhesive foam; chalk ink; dye ink; glossy topcoat (Ranger); sandpaper

Page 84

Spring Break 2006 *Alecia Grimm*

Supplies: Album (SEI); patterned paper (Creative Imaginations, Sonburn, Urban Lily); chipboard letters (Heidi Swapp); chipboard accents (Bazzill, Creative Imaginations); sticker accents (7 Gypsies, Scenic Route); brads; corner rounder; decorative scissors; dye ink; sandpaper; pen; cardstock

Page 86

Carnival *Vicki Boutin*

Supplies: Patterned paper, chipboard stars (Imagination Project); acrylic letter stickers (Junkitz); letter stickers (EK Success, Making Memories); acrylic accents (KI Memories); ticket accent (Daisy D's); ribbon (American Crafts, Michaels, Offray); book ring; chipboard; circle cutter; sandpaper; pen; cardstock

Page 88

Mote Aquarium with Grandpa *Linda Harrison*

Supplies: Patterned paper, accent and letter stickers (Arctic Frog); ribbons (Arctic Frog, Offray); book rings (Karen Foster); pen; cardstock; Day Roman font (Internet download)

Page 90

Butterfly Conservatory *Vicki Boutin*

Supplies: Patterned paper (A2Z Essentials, Daisy D's); chipboard letter (Zsiage); chipboard accents (Daisy D's, Imagination Project); rub-ons (BasicGrey, Creative Imaginations, Me & My Big Ideas, Scenic Route); stickers (EK Success, Heidi Grace, Paper House, Stemma); metal flower (Making Memories); tags (7 Gypsies, Daisy D's, Sassafras Lass); rhinestones; chalk; butterfly templates (Fiskars); pen; cardstock

Page 92

Ft. Wayne Zoo *Greta Hammond*

Supplies: Patterned paper, chipboard letters (Scenic Route); stamp (Gelatins); page tabs (Autumn Leaves); bookplate, rub-ons (Making Memories); decorative tape (7 Gypsies); brads; button; dye ink; label maker; staples; thread

Page 94

Chicago Children's Museum *Courtney Walsh*

Supplies: Album (Maya Road); patterned paper (Scenic Route); letter stickers (Chatterbox); acrylic paint; corner rounder; dye ink; Velcro squares; cardstock; Verdana font (Microsoft)

Page 96

Sea World *Suzy Plantamura*

Supplies: Chipboard album (Rusty Pickle); patterned paper (Creative Imaginations, Crossed Paths, Daisy Bucket, K&Co., Provo Craft, Reminisce); chipboard letters (Heidi Swapp, Me & My Big Ideas); plastic letters (Creative Imaginations, Heidi Swapp); epoxy letters (Me & My Big Ideas); buttons, epoxy stickers (Autumn Leaves); chipboard accents (Technique Tuesday); rub-ons (My Mind's Eye); ribbon (Making Memories, Me & My Big Ideas); rickrack (Doodlebug, Li'l Davis, Me & My Big Ideas); marker

Globetrotter's Paradise

Page 100

Places Scrapbooking Has Taken Me *May Flaum*

Supplies: Patterned paper (Autumn Leaves, Scenic Route); chipboard accent (Scenic Route); letter stickers, clear overlay (Autumn Leaves); digital frame, star border (Two Peas in a Bucket); digital map (Yahoo); flowers, word rub-ons (American Crafts); brad (K&Co.); photo corners (Heidi Swapp); ribbon (Making Memories); tags (7 Gypsies, BasicGrey, Heidi Grace); manila tags, pen; cardstock

Page 102

The Story of Rhyolite *Caroline Ikeji*

Supplies: Patterned paper (Scenic Route); brads, flowers, letter stickers, ribbon (American Crafts); labels (Paper Source); photo corners (Heidi Swapp, KI Memories); stamps (PSX); gaffer tape (7 Gypsies); pigment ink; chipboard book (unknown)

Page 104

Lazy 5 Ranch *Michelle Van Etten*

Supplies: Album, small tag (7 Gypsies); patterned paper (Fancy Pants); chipboard letters (unknown); silk flowers and leaves (Fancy Pants, Prima); textured phrases and tags (All My Memories); transparent bird accent (My Mind's Eye); ribbons (American Crafts, May Arts, Michaels); brads (Queen & Co.); chalk ink; swirl stamp (Autumn Leaves); label maker (Dymo); corner punch; staples; pen; cardstock

Page 106

Mediterranean Summer Cruising *Vicki Boutin*

Supplies: Patterned paper (Cloud 9, Creative Imaginations); chipboard (Daisy D's, Scenic Route); envelopes (Staples); rub-ons (Cloud 9); stamps (Gelatins, Technique Tuesday); dye ink; stickers (Cloud 9, EK Success, Making Memories); metal tag (Creative Imaginations); brads, ribbon (unknown); pen; cardstock

Page 108

Trains *Caroline Ikeji*

Supplies: Digital patterned paper, acrylic stars, alphabet brushes, tags (Designer Digitals); chipboard star (Deluxe Designs); label (7 Gypsies); buttons (American Crafts); ribbons (American Crafts, KI Memories, SEI); book ring; pen; photo quality paper; image editing software (Adobe)

Page 110

Bird's Eye View *Becky Fleck*

Supplies: Accordion album, photo turns (7 Gypsies); die-cut shapes, patterned paper, stickers (Cosmo Cricket); transparencies (My Mind's Eye); brads; ribbons (Shoebox Trims); magnetic tiebacks (BasicGrey); acrylic paint; dye ink; sandpaper; cardstock; Mutlu, Never Writes Back, Nigma fonts (Internet download)

Page 112

Mexico *Alecia Grimm*

Supplies: Album (Scissor Sisters); patterned paper (American Crafts, Paper Salon); letter stickers (K&Co., Making Memories); beads (Mermaid Tears); die-cut stickers (7 Gypsies, Paper House); chipboard accents (Li'l Davis); mesh (Magic Mesh); tag (7 Gypsies); brads; pigment ink; pen; cardstock

Page 114

Paraguay *Alecia Grimm*

Supplies: Suitcase (Paper Source); patterned paper (KI Memories, Rhonna Designs); die-cut accents (My Mind's Eye); pigment ink; rubber stamps (Scrapping Arts); rub-on accents (7 Gypsies); sticker accents (Die Cuts With A View, Li'l Davis, Making Memories); tabs (Heidi Swapp); tag (My Mind's Eye); decoupage medium; souvenirs from Paraguay (artist's own collection)

Pages 116, 118

Architecture Through My Lens *Barb Hogan*

Supplies: Album (Making Memories); patterned paper (7 Gypsies, Anna Griffin, ANW Crestwood, BasicGrey, Crafter's Workshop); ribbon (Michaels); image editing software (Adobe); pigment ink; pen; cardstock; DaVinci font (Internet download)

source GUIDE

The following companies manufacture products featured in this book. Please check your local retailers to find these materials, or go to a company's Web site for the latest product. In addition, we have made every attempt to properly credit the items mentioned in this book. We apologize to any company that we have listed incorrectly, and we would appreciate hearing from you.

7 Gypsies
(877) 749-7797
www.sevengypsies.com

A2Z Essentials
(419) 663-2869
www.geta2z.com

Adobe Systems Incorporated
(800) 833-6687
www.adobe.com

All My Memories
(888) 553-1998
www.allmymemories.com

American Crafts
(801) 226-0747
www.americancrafts.com

Anna Griffin, Inc.
(888) 817-8170
www.annagriffin.com

ANW Crestwood
(973) 406-5000
www.anwcrestwood.com

Arctic Frog
(479) 636-3764
www.arcticfrog.com

Artistic Expressions
(219) 764-5158
www.artisticexpressionsinc.com

Autumn Leaves
(800) 588-6707
www.autumnleaves.com

BasicGrey
(801) 544-1116
www.basicgrey.com

Bazzill Basics Paper
(480) 558-8557
www.bazzillbasics.com

Berwick Offray, LLC
(800) 344-5533
www.offray.com

C & T Publishing
(800) 284-1114
www.ctpub.com

Canson, Inc.
(800) 628-9283
www.canson-us.com

Chatterbox, Inc.
(888) 416-6260
www.chatterboxinc.com

Cloud 9 Design
(866) 348-5661
www.cloud9design.biz

Cosmo Cricket
(800) 852-8810
www.cosmocricket.com

Crafter's Workshop, The
(877) 272-3837
www.thecraftersworkshop.com

Crate Paper
(702) 966-0409
www.cratepaper.com

Creating Keepsakes
(888) 247-5282
www.creatingkeepsakes.com

Creative Imaginations
(800) 942-6487
www.cigift.com

Crossed Paths
(972) 393-3755
www.crossedpaths.net

Daisy Bucket Designs
(541) 289-3299
www.daisybucketdesigns.com

Daisy D's Paper Company
(888) 601-8955
www.daisydspaper.com

Darice, Inc.
(800) 321-1494
www.darice.com

Deluxe Designs
(480) 497-9005
www.deluxecuts.com

Designer Digitals
www.designerdigitals.com

Die Cuts With A View
(801) 224-6766
www.diecutswithaview.com

Doodlebug Design Inc.
(877) 800-9190
www.doodlebug.ws

Dymo
(800) 426-7827
www.dymo.com

EK Success, Ltd.
(800) 524-1349
www.eksuccess.com

Expo International, Inc.
(800) 542-4367
www.expointl.com

Fancy Pants Designs, LLC
(801) 779-3212
www.fancypantsdesigns.com

FiberMark
(802) 257-0365
www.fibermark.com

Fiskars, Inc.
(866) 348-5661
www.fiskars.com

Fontwerks
(604) 942-3105
www.fontwerks.com

Gel•a•tins
(800) 393-2151
www.gelatinstamps.com

Hambly Screen Prints
(408) 496-1100
www.hamblyscreenprints.com

Heidi Grace Designs, Inc.
(866) 348-5661
www.heidigrace.com

Heidi Swapp/Advantus Corporation
(904) 482-0092
www.heidiswapp.com

Imagination Project, Inc.
(888) 477-6532
www.imaginationproject.com

Junkitz
(732) 792-1108
www.junkitz.com

K&Company
(888) 244-2083
www.kandcompany.com

Karen Foster Design
(801) 451-9779
www.karenfosterdesign.com

KI Memories
(972) 243-5595
www.kimemories.com

Li'l Davis Designs
(480) 223-0080
www.lildavisdesigns.com

Magic Mesh
(651) 345-6374
www.magicmesh.com

Magnetic Poetry
(800) 370-7697
www.magneticpoetry.com

Making Memories
(801) 294-0430
www.makingmemories.com

Marcel Schurman/Papyrus
(800) 333-6724
www.schurmanfinepapers.com

Mark Richards Enterprises, Inc.
(888) 901-0091
www.markrichardsusa.com

May Arts
(800) 442-3950
www.mayarts.com

Maya Road, LLC
(214) 488-3279
www.mayaroad.com

me & my BiG ideas
(949) 583-2065
www.meandmybigideas.com

Melissa Frances/Heart & Home, Inc.
(888) 616-6166
www.melissafrances.com

Mermaid Tears
(310) 569-3345
www.mermaidtears.net

Michaels Arts & Crafts
(800) 642-4235
www.michaels.com

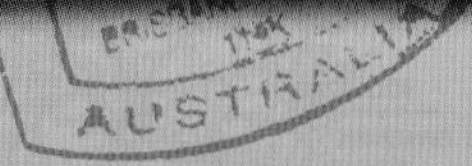

Microsoft Corporation
www.microsoft.com

Mill Hill
www.millhill.com

MOD — My Own Design
(303) 641-8680
www.mod-myowndesign.com

Mustard Moon
(763) 493-5157
www.mustardmoon.com

My Mind's Eye, Inc.
(866) 989-0320
www.mymindseye.com

NRN Designs
(800) 421-6958
www.nrndesigns.com

Nunn Design
(800) 761-3557
www.nunndesign.com

Offray —
see Berwick Offray, LLC

Paper House Productions
(800) 255-7316
www.paperhouseproductions.com

Paper Love Designs —
no longer in business

Paper Salon
(800) 627-2648
www.papersalon.com

Paper Source
(888) 727-3711
www.paper-source.com

Paper Studio
(480) 557-5700
www.paperstudio.com

Paperchase
www.paperchase.co.uk

Plaid Enterprises, Inc.
(800) 842-4197
www.plaidonline.com

Prima Marketing, Inc.
(909) 627-5532
www.primamarketinginc.com

Provo Craft
(800) 937-7686
www.provocraft.com

PSX Design
www.sierra-enterprises.com/psxmain

Queen & Co.
(858) 613-7858
www.queenandcompany.com

QuicKutz, Inc.
(888) 702-1146
www.quickutz.com

Rand McNally
www.randmcnally.com

Ranger Industries, Inc.
(800) 244-2211
www.rangerink.com

Reminisce Papers
(319) 358-9777
www.shopreminisce.com

Rhonna Designs
www.rhonnadesigns.com

Rouge de Garance
www.rougedegarance.com

Rubber Stampede
(800) 423-4135
www.rubberstampede.com

Rusty Pickle
(801) 746-1045
www.rustypickle.com

Sassafras Lass
(801) 269-1331
www.sassafraslass.com

Scenic Route Paper Co.
(801) 225-5754
www.scenicroutepaper.com

Scissor Sisters
(877) 773-7786
www.scissor-sisters.com

Scrapping Arts
(207) 469-0727
www.scrappingarts.com

Scrapworks, LLC/As You Wish Products, LLC
(801) 363-1010
www.scrapworks.com

SEI, Inc.
(800) 333-3279
www.shopsei.com

Shoebox Trims
(303) 257-7578
www.shoeboxtrims.com

SmileMakers
(800) 825-8085
www.smilemakers.com

Sonburn, Inc.
(800) 436-4919
www.sonburn.com

Southworth Company
(800) 225-1839
www.southworth.com

Staples, Inc.
www.staples.com

Stemma — Masterpiece Studios
www.masterpiecestudios.com

Sticker Studio
(888) 244-2083
www.stickerstudio.com

Technique Tuesday, LLC
(503) 644-4073
www.techniquetuesday.com

Teters Floral Product
(800) 999-5996
www.teters.com

Three Bugs in a Rug, LLC
(801) 804-6657
www.threebugsinarug.com

Two Peas in a Bucket
(888) 896-7327
www.twopeasinabucket.com

Urban Lily
www.urbanlily.com

Wal-Mart Stores, Inc.
www.walmart.com

We R Memory Keepers, Inc.
(801) 539-5000
www.weronthenet.com

Wübie Prints
(888) 256-0107
www.wubieprints.com

Yahoo
www.yahoo.com

Zsiage, LLC
(718) 224-1976
www.zsiage.com

INDEX

2-ring albums 66, 74, 76
3-ring albums 44, 70, 80, 88
4-ring albums 72

A Natural Attraction 60-77
Accordion albums 110
Altered book albums 12
Autograph albums 80
A-Z albums 92

Box albums 56

Calendar albums 70
Chipboard albums 32, 38, 50, 52, 54, 68, 74, 76, 90, 96, 102
Circle albums 50, 52, 86, 88, 96
Color-blocking 26
Crackle medium 12

Gatefold albums 46
Globetrotter's Paradise 98-119

Handmade albums 12, 28, 44,62, 72, 100, 108
Hit the Open Road 8-23

Interactive elements 94

Japanese stab binding 62
Journal albums 34, 62
Journaling techniques 16, 52, 54, 68, 86

Life's a Beach 42-59

Manila envelope albums 106
Memorabilia 22, 44, 68, 70
Post-bound albums 10, 14, 30, 36, 84, 112, 114
Postcard albums 54
Pre-made albums 16

Savvy in the City 24-41
Spiral-bound albums 18, 34, 38, 46, 64, 82, 92, 104

Tag albums 54, 90
Ticket to Fun 78-97

Unique shapes/formats 16, 28, 32, 38, 62, 90

Discover more creative ideas for albums and paper crafts with these great titles from Memory Makers Books!

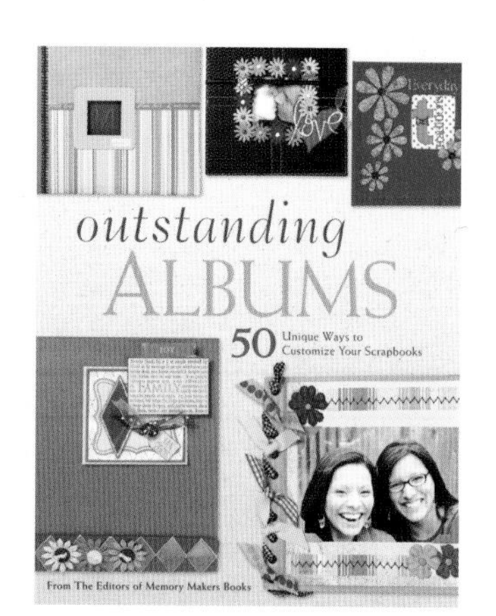

Discover 50 amazing ideas for customizing pre-made albums as well as unique formats for creating handmade albums from scratch.
ISBN-13: 978-1-892127-90-7
ISBN-10: 1-892127-90-3
paperback
112 pages
Z0276

Stretch your supplies beyond scrapbook pages to create beautiful paper crafts such as greeting cards, tags, decorative notebooks, home décor and more.
ISBN-13: 978-1-892127-86-0
ISBN-10: 1-892127-86-5
paperback
128 pages
Z0056

Learn from scrapbook artist Trudy Sigurdson on how to begin a journey into capturing emotion on scrapbook pages through the use of poems, quotes and sayings.
ISBN-13: 978-1-892127-84-6
ISBN-10: 1-892127-84-9
paperback
112 pages
Z0023

These books and other fine Memory Makers Books titles are available from you local art or craft retailer, bookstore or online supplier. Please see page 2 of this book for contact information for Canada, Australia, the U.K. and Europe.